THE
PATTERSON
PRINCIPLES
OF SELLING

revived and revised by

JEFFREY GITOMER

the modern leader of salesmanship
author of **The Sales Bible**

WILEY

JOHN WILEY & SONS, INC.

Published by John Wiley & Sons, Inc., Hoboken, New Jersey.
Published simultaneously in Canada.

For general information on our other products and services, please contact our
Customer Care Department within the United States at (800) 762-2974, outside the
United States at (317) 572-3993 or fax (317) 572-4002.

Wiley also publishes its books in a variety of electronic formats. Some content that
appears in print may not be available in electronic books. For more information
about Wiley products, visit our website at www.Wiley.com.

Library of Congress Cataloging-in-Publication Data:

Gitomer, Jeffrey H.
  The Patterson principles of selling / Jeffrey Gitomer.
     p. cm.
  Includes bibliographical references and index.
  ISBN 0-471-66262-3 (cloth)
  1. Selling. 2. Success in business. 3. Patterson, John Henry, 1844 - 1922.
I. Title.
  HF5438.25.G583 2004
  658.85--dc22

                                                                    2004001724

Printed in the United States of America

10 9 8 7 6 5 4 3 2 1

"People don't like
to be sold,
but they love to buy."

Jeffrey Gitomer, 1989

"If the prospect
understood
the proposition,
he would not have to
be sold; he would
come to buy."

John Patterson, 1889

TABLE OF CONTENTS

A WALK IN THE GRAVEYARD

"People don't like to be sold, but they love to buy" is a registered trademark phrase of mine. It's my sales mantra. I have used it for years.

My research director, Amanda Desrochers, screamed, "Jeffrey! Listen to this!" She read, "'If the prospect understood the proposition, he would not have to be sold; he would come to buy.' It's a Patterson quote." She chortled with delight. "You guys have the same thoughts!"

I was not surprised, but I was amazed (and gratified) at the similarity of our philosophy. And the span of time where so little has changed.

One hundred years separated those statements, but they are philosophically less than a centimeter apart.

There's an old saying that goes, "The more things change, the more they remain the same." Like many sayings, it's old because it's true.

JOHN PATTERSON
President, The National Cash Register Company

This book is your opportunity to learn selling at the feet of John Patterson, the founder and President of The National Cash Register Company, and the original master salesman of America. And keep in mind that these successful principles were created before things like the telephone or the automobile. Paved roads were not yet the order of the day. The Wright Brothers (also from Dayton) had not yet flown. Steam and coal were the predominant power. War veterans were from the Civil War. Wanna travel? Stagecoach or train. The wild West was still wild. No traffic on the freeway. No cars. Edison was cranking on the lightbulb. It was the beginning of the manufacturing revolution in America. And John Patterson decided to take a leadership position.

I got the idea to revive Patterson's principles after doing a program for NCR at their annual sales conferences in Miami and Cannes.

As a sales historian, I had always known of Patterson, but I had no idea of his depth of strategies and achievements. He never wrote a commercial book on selling. "This guy is the Father of American salesmanship,"

I thought to myself. "And his principles are buried."

It was Patterson who created the original personality sales model. It was Patterson who created the first book on how to deal with objections. It was Patterson who held the first sales boot camps. In tents. In fields. Patterson didn't call potential customers prospects or suspects; he referred to them as "probable purchasers." And it was Patterson who coined the word THINK! that everyone credits to Watson and IBM. What people don't know is that Watson worked for Patterson, took it when he left, and used it to help begin the legend of IBM. Think about that.

I called NCR, told them my idea to bring Patterson's principles into the 21st century, and they said "yes" on the phone. Cool. I'd do all the research and discover his original strategies that built a multimillion-dollar empire at the turn of the last century, and convert the strategies to computer and cell phone technology.

Off to Dayton, Ohio.

Amanda and I were going to a barbeque place for dinner. We had arrived in Dayton to do Patterson research for the book at the historical society. The restaurant had a 20-minute wait. I decided to take a walk around the neighborhood.

Three blocks later, we came to an old building that looked like a castle split in half with a gate in the middle. "It's a graveyard," I said. "Let's go check it out." I know this sounds goofy, but it was a beautiful place.

The weather cooperated. Cloudy on the verge of a storm. Dusk. Real cemetery weather. There was a car at the gate. Security at a graveyard? Everyone's already dead. I asked the guard if we could enter. "We're about to close, you'll have to exit on the other side of the Welcome Center."

"No problem," I assured him. "Anyone famous buried here?" "The Wright Brothers," he bragged. "Cool," I said. "Anyone else?" "Here's a map," he offered. "Is John Patterson buried here?" I asked. "Sure is. He's in Area nine at the Patterson knoll." He pointed.

I grabbed the map and searched. Found it. As we started walking, it began to drizzle. The only thing missing was a vampire. Giant trees made it light and dark at the same time. It was a huge undulating park with thousands of grave markers. Some as ornate as I've ever seen. Some 50 feet tall.

We found dates back to the early 1800s.

"Over here!" I yelled as I spotted what I thought was the Patterson gravesite. A huge marble arch marked the spot for the Patterson family. About a hundred names on it. On one wall was a brief bio of John, but I couldn't find his actual stone. Every Patterson family member had the same headstone. Smaller than a ten-pound sack of sugar. "Found it!" I screamed. Suddenly I went silent. I just stood on his grave imagining what he was like.

And then a flood of emotion came over me as I imagined the struggle, the risk, the creativity, the pioneering, the leadership, the setbacks, the victory, and every conceivable episode of business life when ultimate success occurs. The vision.

One hundred and eighteen years after his NCR adventure began, as I stood on the grave of John Patterson, an energy ran through my body that told me I was meant to be there. Ever get a feeling like that? Powerful and frightening at the same time.

I was inspired. I was energized. I was ready to take on this century-old task as though I was chosen for it.

Rain was falling as we left. "Pretty cool, huh?" I meekly offered to Amanda. "Unreal. What were the chances of this happening?" she said. "I wonder if it was a long shot or a predetermined one?"

Looking at the sky and the skyline, I said, "Serendipity, I've been told, is God's way of remaining anonymous."

I have chosen, and I have been chosen, to share this information. To take the principles, philosophies, and sales strategies of John Patterson, and memorialize them for the 21st century.

When you read them, you will find as I did that they are as (or more) valid today as they were then. Take them for yourself. Take them for your sales. Take them to the bank.

JEFFREY GITOMER
Chief executive salesman

FATHER OF AMERICAN SALESMANSHIP?

John Patterson was a visionary. He was a thinker; he was a risk-taker; he was a reader; he was an entrepreneur; he was a teacher; he was a student; and he was a salesman. Certainly the best salesman of his time. Arguably the best salesman of all time. Patterson's success was due to his ability to blend the emotion that makes the sale with the logic that figures out the reasoning behind it. He had the perfect blend of logic and emotion. Forming opinions or justifying decisions leans toward being logical, but Patterson understood that the process of buying was an emotional one.

He knew it. *And* he taught it.

Not just a businessman, Patterson was the creator of most of the practices that distinguish modern American business from all other businesses in the world. Not just a salesman, he was the founder of modern salesmanship. Not just a speaker, he was among the most effective of public demonstrators. Not just a financier, he was the chief exponent of getting money by spending money. Not just a manufacturer, he was the originator of the modern American factory. Not just a judge or a picker of men, he was the father of organized business and the developer of more business leaders than any other man of his time. Not just a man of commanding personality, he was a rare leader of men -- equally sure of himself in threatened defeat or in expected victory.

He is salesmanship's father because of ...

the strategies he created.

the methods he pioneered.

the manner in which he transferred his genius to his team.

and their track record of success to prove it.

He is salesmanship's father because he was the first person who realized a customer was more likely to complete a transaction through buying than selling. He created the original "pull through" model. He pioneered sales training. He taught his men to adapt and harmonize with the *"probable purchaser"* (which we now erroneously call the "prospect"). He inspired his people with ideas that worked. And he backed his salespeople with advertising and promotion so that the NCR brand of cash register was by far the machine of choice.

But far and away, the overwhelming evidence of his genius was his concept of …

"Creating the demand for a receipt, rather than just trying to sell the concept of a cash register."

WHERE DID JOHN PATTERSON GET HIS
CONCEPTS AND STRATEGIES?

He read.

Patterson regarded a good book as a great mental possession. Only books worthy of being read again and again were to be found in his private library. All of his books are marked and underlined cover to cover. Whenever new knowledge appeared, Patterson underlined it, bookmarked it, studied it, **and put it into practice**.

Many underlined passages in his books show the essence of the message that captured his attention. Books helped to shape the man and the empire he built. Patterson believed that a good book was not the plaything for the idle hour, but a veritable means for generating power.

He read. *And* he generated power.

AUTHOR'S PERSONAL NOTE: *The guy before Napoleon Hill.* The person Napoleon Hill emulated was Orison Swett Marden. He was the original positive-attitude genius of the 20th century. Lately I have been buying every Marden book I can get my hands on. **(For a complete list of Marden books, go to www.gitomer.com and enter the words MARDEN BOOKS into the GitBit box.)**

About two years ago, I purchased a bunch of books from the original John Patterson library; most of them were on longevity, plus a few biographies. I was perusing the books last week to complete this work and decided to look at every book that I owned of Patterson's. I pulled out the title, *He Can Who Thinks He Can* by Orison Swett Marden. My blood ran cold. It is a first edition book published in 1908 and I realized we had yet one more thing in common. Smiled. And went about my business.

I carry the Marden book from Patterson's library with me now and read a page or two a day.

I especially read the parts that Patterson underlined. As usual, he found the gems. Here are a few:

QUOTES UNDERLINED BY THE HAND OF JOHN PATTERSON TAKEN FROM THE BOOK

HE CAN WHO THINKS HE CAN

BY ORISON SWETT MARDEN
PUBLISHED IN 1908

Every child should be taught to expect success.

———————

People do not realize the immense value
of utilizing spare minutes.

———————

Multitudes of people, enslaved by bad physical habits,
are unable to get their best selves into their work.

———————

Some of the greatest men in history never discovered themselves
until they lost everything but their pluck and grit.

———————

Almost anybody can resolve to do a great thing;
it is only the strong, determined character that puts
the resolve into execution.

———————

No substitute has ever yet been discovered for honesty.

———————

Happiness is a condition of mind.

———————

Resolve that you will be a man of ideas,
always on the lookout for improvement.

———————

Power gravitates to the man who knows how and why.

———————

There is no word in the English language
more misused and abused than luck.

**Want the complete list? Go to www.gitomer.com, register if you are
a first-time user, and enter the word MARDEN in the GitBit box.**

PRINCIPLES ARE DRIVEN BY TRUTH

I have chosen to call Patterson's sales philosophies and strategies *"principles"* because they are truths that are up to you to implement into your sales life.

I would much rather do business with someone who is principle-driven than money-driven. Money-driven people have a few bucks, but focus on the money aspect of the sale rather than the customer aspect of the sale. And you can smell them like bad milk.

A principle-driven person has wealth. And that wealth is not just in money. It's in reputation, in the actions that they take, their personal pride, and not just their success, but their fulfillment. A person who lives by their principles is much more likely to be fulfilled when they are sitting there counting their money. Everyone counts their money. The question, is how do you feel when you know the total? Get it?

Being a person of principle means that you are self-guided. And in that self-guiding way, you will come to inspire yourself.

The Patterson Principles of Selling are more than 100 years old. They have a history of success. All of them are easily understood. None of them break any of your company's rules. Each of them can be mastered with some hard work. And together these principles encompass an approach to the sales process that will lead you to success this day, this month, this year, and this lifetime.

THE
EVOLUTION AND POWER OF THE RECEIPT

Never forget the genius associated with the philosophy: **Patterson did not sell the register, rather he created the need and the demand for a receipt.** This may be the most powerful business strategy of the 19th and 20th centuries. Take a minute to ponder how you might use that philosophy to build your business. What demands are you creating? Who is calling you to buy?

Add to this incredible reality that the receipt is one of the most powerful pieces of paper in the world. Every receipt has its own power. It's your PROOF of purchase and ownership. And EVERY purchase is now accompanied by one. Thanks to John Patterson.

Receipts not only prove you bought it. They prove you own it, can return it, can exchange it, can get a warranty enforced, can resell it, can get reimbursed for it, can deduct it from your taxes, and much, much more. In many cases you need to show your receipt to exit a store thirty seconds after you just made the purchase.

You save receipts for years. They often outlive the very product you bought.

Think of how often you use your receipts ... they are documents, they are the reminders marking the passage of your time and your money. Receipts are the one constant in business for the last 100 years. *Would you like your receipt in the bag?*

The receipt is the only thing in business that has remained intact. A receipt is the "Prize" because without it, you have lost.

Banking and checking accounts give receipts for transactions. Your cancelled check or credit card statement is your receipt. A receipt is not just a proof of purchase -- it's a recorded transaction. Proof of payment, with clerk, date, time, etc. It's a valuable document of who did what, when they did it, and how much was involved.

Want your money back? Better have your receipt. IRS knocking at your door? Better have your receipts.

*"**Do you want a receipt with that?**"* came way before
*"**Do you want fries with that?**"*

NCR promotional photo used in the early 1900s.

"A receipt, like a deed, is proof of title
to property."   — *1912 quote from a
National Cash Register brochure*

"Try to get a refund without one."
        — *Jeffrey Gitomer*

THE EVOLUTION OF *THE PRIMER*
THE FIRST SALES TRAINING MANUAL

John Patterson did not just believe in the power of training, he lived the essence of it. Early on he realized that training was the link to infinite sales.

The first NCR sales script, "How I Sell A National Cash Register," which became known as *The Primer*, contained instructions on what salesmen should say during a sale, and what they were to do while saying it. *The Primer* covered the factors that were common to every sale.

It divided the sale into 4 parts:
1. The approach to the probable purchaser
2. The demonstration of the register
3. How to overcome objections
4. How to close the sale

This sequence of ideas became the steps to a sale. The first Primer was introduced in June of 1887 at the agents' convention.

It left out a few steps, but hey -- not bad for 120 years old.

The Primer began when Joe Crane, Patterson's brother-in-law and their best salesman, was asked to sit in on a meeting devoted to the discussion of prices. At the end of the meeting, Crane stated that the price was alright and the product was good, but that they didn't know how to sell it. **Crane saw that the salesmen were selling in the purchaser's environment.** That was where the problem started. Here they were more susceptible to distractions. Sales distractions. It was much better to take the purchaser elsewhere.

This idea worked phenomenally for Crane, and Patterson wanted his salesmen to follow Crane's lead. Crane said the same thing, word for word, during each demonstration to his probable purchasers.

At first, Patterson thought this would become monotonous and tiresome, but Crane replied, "It has never got monotonous yet. The reason it is not monotonous is because it is to different people every time." Crane presented Patterson with one of his demonstrations, after which Patterson stated, "I will call the stenographer; you dictate this to him and get it typewritten."

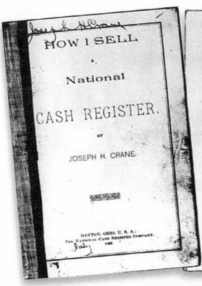

1887 edition

1923 edition

"We progress through change."

— *Patterson's favorite quote*

Patterson made copies and sent them to all of his sales agents (12 at that time) with a note: "Crane sells more machines than any of you fellows, and he sells them this way. I suggest that you all learn this." He published it and called it *How I Sell A National Cash Register* by Joseph H. Crane.

After reading the script, Patterson's men felt there was "too much Crane in it" so he revised the text and published it as the NCR *Primer*.

The Primer was the first documented sales training tool.

Patterson felt the use of a standardized presentation would make a good salesman a better one. His men had to memorize this *Primer* word for word. Patterson's thinking was that if his men knew *The Primer* word for word, and said it so many times, they would never forget what they said during any demonstration.

Was it the best system in the world? -- No, but it WORKED. And it worked well in those times. Even though you don't want to sound mechanical, there's something to be said for repeating a formula that works.

Patterson tested his men's ability to repeat the text on a continuing basis. If someone replied in a "schoolboy" fashion or did not recite it naturally or spontaneously, Patterson would send him off to Dayton for a course of training. When the salesman had committed *The Primer* to memory, no interruptions could throw him off track.

The reputation of Patterson is not a benevolent one. He was strict, and all business at all times. And, let's face it, there weren't many distractions in those days. No TV, no computers, no cars, no shopping malls, and his wife was not much of a looker (just kidding). Newspapers, magazines, the mail, and rumors were the primary methods of information transfer.

Concentration on a single purpose was easier to say the least, and Patterson had an obsession for this.

As *The Primer* grew, so did the selling strategies and concepts. *The Primer* addressed everything from dressing to closing. And it detailed the first personality and situational selling methodology. It became their bible of selling (not to be confused with *The Sales Bible* that appeared 100 years later).

By 1923, *The Primer* was mature. It had expanded into two volumes: A "Manual" and "Selling Helps."

MANUAL FOR NCR SALESMEN, 1923 EDITION

This manual contained selling methods used by the most successful sales representatives. It was divided into five parts …

> **NCR Salesmanship:** An NCR salesman was made up of five components: health, honesty, knowledge, courage, and hard work.

> **Suggestions for Study:** Three areas to focus on were the need for the register, the salesman's actual knowledge of the register, and the selling process.

> **Store Systems and Their Weak Points:** Patterson wanted each of his salesmen to be familiar with the various store systems in use and the weak points of each. Knowing the weak points strengthened the sale.

> **The Value of National Cash Register Functions:** The greatest VALUE a register delivered was the PRINTED RECEIPT, along with a detailed strip, and automatic and multiple cash drawers.

> **The Selling Plan:**
> This section discussed the five steps to making a sale:
>
> > **1.** Interesting the merchant
> >
> > **2.** Explaining the register
> >
> > **3.** Closing the sale
> >
> > **4.** Installing the register
> >
> > **5.** Serving the merchant

The manual ended with a lesson on the value and importance of keeping physically fit, and a chart detailing the "50 ways I can improve myself." Patterson did not think in terms of profit, like most salesmen. Instead, he thought in terms of the good the cash register would bring to the probable purchaser. He felt that if his salesman could not sell his product, there must be something wrong with the salesman, not the product. To him, personal appearance was everything. He insisted all his men be clean-shaven, dressed sharp, shoes polished, and be healthy, active, awake, and prosperous. If his men followed these 50 ways, they would be on the road to personal and professional success.

Physically	Mentally
① Simple food, quality, quantity.	① Think sanely.
② Regularity in eating and sleep.	② Learn from mental superiors.
③ Masticate; leave table hungry.	③ Learn to listen attentively.
④ We are a part of all we have eaten.	④ Read best newspapers and books.
⑤ Exercise, five minutes, three times daily.	⑤ Improve the memory.
⑥ Air—most important.	⑥ Concentrate.
⑦ Sunlight, artificial light.	⑦ Don't worry unnecessarily.
⑧ Water inside and outside.	⑧ Be systematic.
⑨ Loose clothing.	⑨ Weigh both sides.
⑩ Early to sleep; get plenty.	⑩ Avoid inferior minds.

50 Ways I Can Improve Myself

Morally	Financially	Socially

① Right is right, wrong is wrong.	① Increase my earnings.	① Avoid bad associates.
② Be truthful.	② Decrease unnecessary expense.	② Select helpful friends.
③ Ignore precedent if wrong.	③ Save money, U. S. Postal Bank.	③ Think alone.
④ Seek elevating recreation.	④ Money makes money.	④ Learn to be happy alone.
⑤ Don't deceive yourself.	⑤ Invest— don't gamble.	⑤ Family best company.
⑥ Learn to say "no."	⑥ Make family budget.	⑥ Work out, alone, my problems.
⑦ Live up to your principles.	⑦ Hard work.	⑦ Avoid so-called society.
⑧ Avoid temptation.	⑧ Study the business.	⑧ Entertain economically.
⑨ Form good habits.	⑨ Pay cash for everything.	⑨ Stand well with neighbors.
⑩ Have a constitution.	⑩ Increase credit balance.	⑩ Do some welfare work.

The NCR Archive at the Montgomery Historical Society

The graphic on the right is a "morph" of two of the classic Patterson images from The Primer. *It's telling you what exercise you need to do to be both physically AND mentally ready to succeed.*

Selling Helps for NCR Salesmen, 1923 Edition

Patterson believed the real reason a merchant didn't buy was because he did not know the benefits a cash register would bring to his business. Because of this, the merchant raised objections and asked questions. *The Primer* created dialogue examples of the most frequently asked questions and objections, along with answers that had been successful to members in the selling force. The topics covered in this manual were as old as they are modern:

Price:
"Your price is too high."

Excuses for Delay:
"I want to think about it."

Temptation:
"My clerks are all honest, they would never steal."

Interested in a Small Register:
"A single drawer register is all I need."

Receipt:
"The clerk will not give out the receipt."

Allowance (trade-in) **Too Small:**
"Your allowance for my old register is not high enough."

Charge Business:
"Seventy percent of my business is charge. I am not interested in your cash register."

I Am Satisfied with My Present System:
"Our present system is fast enough."

One hundred years later, the SAME excuses still pervade the selling process.

Want the Patterson 1923 and the Gitomer 2003 answers to these excuses? Go to www.gitomer.com, register if you are a first-time user, and enter the words SELLING HELPS in the GitBit box.

Also included in "Selling Helps" were experiences and stories from NCR salesmen, how to approach a probable purchaser, a history of the cash register, its ten stages of development, and an article written by Patterson about why he truly felt the need for a receipt. This book captured the essence of what to do in the real world from people who were doing it every day.

Each volume of *The Primer* was numbered and assigned to a salesman. If he quit or was terminated, he had to turn it in. That statement alone shows you what power and respect they gave the document.

When I first read *The Primer* in the Montgomery County Historical Society where the Patterson archives are preserved, it was like I was reading the Holy Grail or the Talmud.

Ancient sales philosophies, methods, and strategies that are still valid today

---

The pages that follow are
The Patterson Principles of Selling.
They have been extracted from
The Primer and other writings
by and about Patterson.

I have taken the liberty
to change a few words
as they apply to sales
100 years later.

WHAT IS A PRINCIPLE YOU ASK?

A principle is a concept. A strategy. A thought that when understood, practiced, and implemented into your sales process becomes part of your philosophy, rather than simply a technique. Principles are the highest form of action and self-belief. "Give me liberty or give me death!" is a principle.

I have uncovered 32 major sales principles of John Patterson.

I believe they capture the essence of what he preached and practiced. I have also added my 21st-century adaptations and concepts to implement these strategies into your selling quest for success. Many of them spill over from sales to life. All the better. All the more powerful.

I have taken the liberty to adjust a word here and there without violating the Patterson way of thinking … our philosophies are so similar it's scary. And I have added one of my own. It's the .5 in the 32.5 Principles. It's the one that glues the others together. But the real question you're asking right now is:

"Hey Gitomer, what's in this for me?"

HERE'S WHAT YOU WILL FIND FOR YOU AS YOU READ EACH PRINCIPLE ...

THE PATTERSON PRINCIPLES

THE QUOTES (one from John, one from me -- and an occasional one from someone else relevant). The quotes emphasize the principle.

THE DESCRIPTION AND EXPLANATION OF THE PRINCIPLE

 THINK!
The real world application process to make you THINK -- The word THINK! will challenge you to do just that. There will be "thinks" to think about. Questions to ask yourself. You will find a THINK icon after each principle to help you understand how to think about the concept and adapt it for yourself.

 PP: **The real world application process to help you understand the mind of the probable purchaser** -- **PP** will tell you what you can do with the principle. How you can act on it. How it will help you make a sale.

AND OF COURSE, IN THE TRUE PATTERSON FASHION, THERE WILL BE AN EXERCISE

 EXERCISE: Something you can do right now to begin mastering the principle. Convert the ideas presented into personal achievement for you. In other words, turning thoughts into actions.

THE PROBABLE PURCHASER

Patterson's selling philosophy was centered around the concept of referring to a prospect as a probable purchaser -- thus defining the prospect and your attitude towards him or her in the SAME breath! So powerful. It's the biggest sales aha I've had since I earned my first commission back in 1963 (yeah, 1963). **Probable purchaser is also referenced in the book as PP.**

To me,
PP is as powerful
a sales philosophy
as I have EVER
seen or read --
and it's well over
a hundred years old --
AND NO ONE USES IT.

Patterson could have used words like *prospect, possible, prospective,* and *potential,* but in his positive-attitude thought process, he not only assumed the sale, he put word-thoughts into the minds of his salespeople so they would constantly reinforce their own belief system. *Probable purchaser* is a classic lost element of the Patterson Principles of Selling that will not only be resurrected here, but that you can employ every day as you seek success.

HERE ARE THE 32.5 PATTERSON PRINCIPLES OF SELLING ...

These principles
by themselves
will not just give
you a sale today.

They will enhance
your selling process,
and give you
sales forever.

1. Think!

"Think and act — two words of progress."
— *John H. Patterson*

"Thinking. An action that very few
people take the time to do."
— *Jeffrey Gitomer*

The word **THINK!** will carry you through the rest of the book.

An action that very few people take the time to do. And a lifetime opportunity to stay ahead and succeed.

Patterson believed that progress was the result of thought.

The phrase **Think!** was used as a motivational tool for Patterson's salesmen as well as the rest of the workers within the company.

In 1911, after NCR's one-millionth register was sold, a pocket-sized book was printed for the salesmen as a motivational reminder. The book was entitled, *THINK!* and contained brief passages about what some of the greatest inventors were doing for the world at that time.

"Think of what a great thing Thomas A. Edison did when he thought of the incandescent light" is an example of those passages. At the end of the book, Patterson showed how thought made the cash register a common item in each business for over one million merchants.

The word Think! was intended for the salesmen and for the merchants. The object was to get the salesmen to think of better ways to earn sales and referrals, and get the merchants to think about what the register could do for their business.

Thinking, like any other action, is a discipline. You decide your own outcome based on your desire and self-determination.

Realize early on in this writing that every principle takes action on your part to master it. And that "thought" will be the backbone of your ideas and their implementation -- your actions to succeed.

Twelve things to Think! about every day:

How can I uncover new customers?

How can I become a better presenter?

How does my customer profit from using my product?

How did I better myself today?

What did I learn new?

How can I serve better?

Is my attitude better today than it was yesterday?

Are my customers loyal today?

How am I investing my time today?

Did I get a referral today?

Did I give a referral today?

Did I work on my legacy today?

THINK about taking action on each of these twelve thoughts.

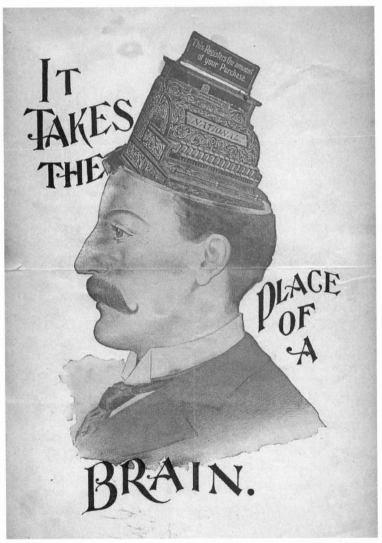

This image appeared on the back cover
of the June 1894 issue of *The Hustler*.

Most people have no idea how to spend time in thought. Try writing your thoughts as you come up with them.

AUTHOR'S NOTE: I have been writing my thoughts for eleven years. It's not just thinking -- it's capturing your thoughts and turning them into reality.

What have you been thinking about?

How have you turned those thoughts into actions?

How do you know when a thought is complete? Answer: You don't. If you think you have a good thought or idea, just try it. Part of converting thoughts into actions is risk. The best way to look at risk is as an opportunity to achieve and grow.

Exercise: Set aside THINK! time -- make a THINK appointment every day, even if it's only 15 minutes. Decide in advance what you want to think about and what solutions you're looking for. I know, it sounds hokey -- **but here's the gold:**

Write ideas no matter how far-fetched they sound -- just write for ten minutes straight. Your stream-of-consciousness thinking will net you some amazing results.

THINK!
Do it for a week.
The results will be so amazing,
you'll do it for a lifetime.

2. Self-belief ...

The Most Convincing Characteristic of a Salesperson

"If the salesman himself has faith in the honesty of his goods, he will have little trouble in convincing his customers."

— Frank Farrington
(This quote was taken from an
underlined book in Patterson's library.)

"Self-belief is a most convincing characteristic to others, and THE most convincing characteristic to yourself."

— Jeffrey Gitomer

"Believe in yourself and your product."

— 1921 Manual for NCR Salesmen

First, and above all, Patterson trained his salesmen to believe in themselves as salesmen before learning anything else about the selling process. The first page of the 1923 sales manual explained the importance of self-belief. The manual read, "You must believe in yourself. You must believe that you can do what you undertake or you can never do it. Success in selling is up to each one of us individually."

Self-belief is the most convincing sales characteristic that must be mastered. You must believe you are the best salesman in the world, and you must believe you work for the best company in the world. And you must believe you are selling the best product in the world.

If you don't believe, no one else will either.

**Before you can sell anyone else,
you must be sold on your company,
you must be sold on your product, and
you must be sold on yourself.**

What do you believe in?

How can you strengthen
your self-belief?

Do you realize that self-belief is
tied to your degree of success?

In order for a sale to take place, three things must be present.
One -- you gotta believe that you work for the greatest
company in the world. Two -- you gotta believe that you have
the greatest product in world. And three -- you gotta believe
that you are the greatest person in the world.

The key words are:
"You Gotta Believe."

Strong belief will make you a more innovative, creative salesperson
with a burning drive and desire to help the other person buy --
and that's a big difference from a burning drive and desire to sell
something. *People don't like to be sold, but they love to buy.*

Exercise: Want an instant lesson? Go out and buy a copy of
The Little Engine That Could. Or go to your kid's room and get
the copy full of crayon marks. Read it regularly. **It's not just a
book for kids, it's a philosophy for a lifetime.**

3. Positive Mental Attitude Is Determined by You, Not Others.

"Success in selling is up to the attitude within each one of us individually."

— *John H. Patterson*

"The way you dedicate yourself to the way you think is the definition of attitude, either positive or negative. The only difference is the choice you make about the way you think."

— *Jeffrey Gitomer*

Your mental attitude is your motivation.

Positive mental attitude is the motivation and inspiration that feeds off of your self-belief. Success in sales and success in service starts with a positive attitude.

Attitude is defined as the way you dedicate yourself to the way you think. Think negative or think positive is a choice and a process. **Negative** is (unfortunately) an instinctive process. **Positive** is a learned self-discipline that must be studied and practiced every day.

When you're giving any form of communication or presentation, your attitude will shine through.

Sometimes your personal sun is not shining. Things may be wrong with your family, finances, or your health.

If you let this transcend into your sales presentation and your customer communications, the consequence is low or no sales.

The result will be that you blame others for your own inability to separate your attitude from your events.

You become what you think about all day long.

— Earl Nightingale

Want to start making an attitude change? Take attitude actions. To achieve a POSITIVE attitude, you must take physical, verbal, and mental ACTIONS. Every day. Read two pages from a positive book at the start of every day. **For a listing of positive reading books, go to www.gitomer.com and enter the words SALES PILLS in the GitBit box.**

Exercise: The EYE Can. Cut out eyes from a magazine and glue them to a tin can. If you think you can't, look at the eye (I) can and know that you can succeed.

4. Boot Camp Separates the Salesman from the Wanna-be Salesman.

"Industry is cheap. It is laziness that costs. It has cost many a bright man a bright career."

— *John H. Patterson*

"Sales is survival, the best-prepared are most likely to survive."

— *Jeffrey Gitomer*

Survival tactics, while they may not always be employed, must be mastered so that they can be implemented whenever the situation arises. This is not simply how to find water in the desert; this is how to beat the competition. How to sell when times are tough or how to win in any struggle or any environment.

Survival is not about saving your hide; survival is about mastering a circumstance or environment and emerging victorious.

Basic training includes physical, mental, and psychological self-discipline. Intense basic training is a requirement for success in any sport, particularly the sport of selling.

Patterson put his men through his own personal boot camp in order to ensure he was hiring only the BEST men for his team.

He didn't view the hiring process as hiring a salesman. Rather, he hired men whom he planned to train in sales.

The "basic training" that Patterson put his men through was more like army basic training.

And he made people go through his basic training program in a tent, in a field, with hundreds of others, rain or shine, hot or cold, BEFORE they were hired. This way Patterson knew that he was hiring strong salesmen in every sense of the word.

His ability to attract men was legendary. People were willing to come (and they came by the hundreds) to a Patterson camp and prove they could qualify to be an NCR salesman before they ever earned a nickel. In 1900, starting pay was $4 a week. But they didn't have to worry about gas money. There weren't any cars yet.

The NCR Archive at the Montgomery Historical Society

Tents at Sugar Camp training site, c1924.

Have you ever noticed that some people just look more alive than others? In my experience I have found that people who combine physical and mental exercise seem more alert and ready to sell and serve. And by coincidence also seem to be the ones who can make their enthusiasm and self-confidence contagious.

Customers seem to receive healthy salespeople and their information in a more positive manner. I guess you could refer to it as the total package of brains, brawn, and beauty. And that equates to believability and buying from the probable purchaser.

> "Selling is a blend of mental and physical symphonic motions that perform in harmony with each other. When your mind and body aren't working in unison, the performance is off-key."
>
> — *Jeffrey Gitomer*

How much ENERGY are you putting into your basic training?

How DEDICATED are you to getting better at selling?

Probably not enough! What is your personal boot camp? How would you describe it? How do you discipline yourself on an ongoing basis? What is your daily agenda? Consider this: What would Patterson add to YOUR daily agenda? How well would you do in his boot camp? Would you have survived the tasks at hand? Or would you have complained, "no cable TV?"

"Boot camp is a fight for the fit. Rigorous training is the lifeblood for future sales (and business) success."
— *John H. Patterson*

"You can't teach an old dog new tricks. OK, so don't train old dogs. Same with salespeople." — *Jeffrey Gitomer*

Exercise must be both physical and mental.

 Exercise: Train mentally for 30 minutes a day. Give yourself that gift for a lifetime.

Working out can improve your business game. Sweat a little. Regular physical exercise can ... Reduce your level of anxiety. Help you manage stress more effectively. Improve your positive self-esteem and confidence. Help you relax. Help you sleep more restfully. And ... can teach you about goal-setting, dedication, and personal achievement.

There is a link between physical and mental fitness.

Blood flow to the brain caused by physical exercise leads to clearer thoughts and better decisions.

How can you NOT find 30 minutes 5 times a week to fit all those physical benefits into your mental sales plan?

"Ill health affects the mental ability, spoils the disposition, and handicaps one's progress."

— *John H. Patterson*

"Your physical status may be robbing you of a chance for fiscal sales success."

— *Jeffrey Gitomer*

NCR sales agents' training class, July 11, 1924.
Can you imagine your sales team out in the field doing this? For a week? In the rain?

> "People could not work at their best
> unless their health was of the best."
> — *John H. Patterson*

> "Looking successful is a big part of
> achieving success. It starts with the
> look of health." — *Jeffrey Gitomer*

5. Survival Is a Combination of Knowing and Doing.

"If there ever comes a time in this business when courage will not be necessary, when it will not be necessary for us to fight against obstacles, I shall know that it is time to put up the shutters, turn off the power, and draw the fires for all times."

— John H. Patterson

"All salespeople know what to do. Problem is, they don't do it."

— Jeffrey Gitomer

"The biggest reason people don't succeed is that they don't expose themselves to existing information." says Jim Rohn. And I add to that -- "Therefore, they don't believe in themselves enough (lack the confidence) to succeed."

It's not so important that you **want** to succeed -- it's critical you know **why** you want to succeed -- and what has **prevented** you from achieving your success to date? What **belief system and game plan** do you need to put in place to gain that success?

It's easy to lose self-belief, if the one you've got in place is weak due to poor knowledge and lack of determination.

It's easy to fail at sales if you have never told yourself (sold yourself) the real reason you want sales success in the first place. Not earning money for money's sake -- *but the real reason you want the money, and what you'll do with it once you get it.*

How do you continue to educate yourself?

Are you at home filling your brain with useless television reruns? Or are you making the most of your time and STUDYING to make yourself a better person, a better SALESperson? What have you done in the last day, week, or month to expand your knowledge?

How much time do you dedicate to your own personal achievement? Answer: Not enough. Here's a few painful questions to ponder.

1. How many books have you read on salesmanship in the last year?

2. How many books have you read on positive attitude in the last year?

3. How many books have you read on creativity in the last year?

4. How many hours did you waste watching television last week?

5. Do you get paid for watching TV? Why are you watching?

6. Could you convert or invest some of your "TV hours" into reading hours?

7. How many sales or personal development tapes do you listen to in your car?

8. How many hours of radio drivel do you listen to in the car?

9. How many hours could you convert or invest from drivel to knowledge?

10. What would that conversion be worth?

10.5 What price are you paying for not converting?

Survival is a combination of knowing and doing. What do you **KNOW**? What are you **DOING**?

 Knowing Exercise: Why do you want to succeed? Answer the question and each time you answer it, add the question "why?" again -- after four or five levels, you'll have the real why.

 Doing Exercise: What is preventing you from doing what you want to do?

 Survival Exercise: Think about what you would do if you lost two of your best customers. Make a plan to prevent it before it becomes a reality.

What do you know? How are you turning that knowledge into money?

Patterson presenting to the "I Will" club, 1913.

"The best way to teach is through the
eye. It is hard to retain what we hear,
but a man remembers what he sees."

— John H. Patterson

"If you want to be great, learn how to
get there."

— Jeffrey Gitomer

6. Studying ...
the First Discipline
of Knowledge.

"There are some young fellows who apparently think salesmanship is a thing that they will someday find somewhere ready-made."

— *John H. Patterson*

"You don't get great at sales in a day, you get great at sales day by day."

— *Jeffrey Gitomer*

The word "studying" is a misnomer. It's actually personal development and knowledge expansion. Education. Awareness. And the dedication to want to learn.

The difference between reading and studying is intensity, focus, and repetition.

To master salesmanship, you must continually repeat messages and practice by doing in order to master the principles and the fundamentals that will lead to success.

Studying is defined as the continuing self-discipline to achieve sales greatness.

On-the-job training is one of the most important facets of a successful company.

You never stop learning, so why should you stop training to be your best? Top athletes are constantly training to perfect their game and stay at peak performance. Top salesmen need to do the same.

Are you spending or investing your time?

How many hours a day do you spend in front of the television? How is that helping your success? What is going to help your success more ... watching 30 minutes of reruns, or dedicating 30 minutes to reading a book that will help the most important person in the world ... YOU?

Training is an everyday occurrence.

Did you study to be a salesman or did you just think it would happen overnight? Selling is a science. An acquired skill. The salesperson who you thought was born to sell painstakingly developed the traits and characteristics to do so, and then went about learning and applying the science of selling.

Think about how you learn: When you were in high school or college, how did you study for exams? How did you learn your material? Notecards? Study groups? Reading? Being quizzed? Cram? Cheat? Take notes? Those habits are still with you.

If you want to build wealth, first build a wealth of knowledge!

Selling is a learned skill, acquired by people with the attitude, aptitude, fortitude, desire, and persistence to succeed.

All of these skills are your personal development skills that must be incorporated with your sales skills. The formula is real simple. If you believe in your product, your service, your company, and yourself; if you work on yourself, reading the above subjects that you never learned in school; and you study the fundamentals of sales from a book entitled *The Sales Bible* (by me), you will begin to develop a self-confidence from your own success.

Help yourself first! If your company does not have adequate training, create your own plan. All the information you need to succeed beyond your wildest dreams already exists. The problem is, you're not exposing yourself to it.

Have you got the desire to learn the skills needed to succeed? Hint: 50% of that desire comes from loving what you do.

Exercise: Self-test AND game plan

— Do I spend 15 minutes a day reading or listening to sales information?

— Do I know how other people's jobs at my office affect my job and my performance?

— Do I read the trade magazines of our company's industry and the trade magazines of our top five customers' industries?

— Do I attend our industry's annual trade show?

— Do I belong to Toastmasters?

— Where's your training "road map" taking you?

Here's an idea! Read about, study, or listen to one new sales technique each day, and before the end of the day, try that technique out at least once. By trying it, you'll see the real world application of what you thought might work.

Bonus: If you do one technique a day, at the end of the year, you'll have roughly 250 new techniques and still have your weekends free.

And at the end of five years, you'll be a world-class expert.

"Business is nothing but teaching."
> — *John H. Patterson*

"Invest time, don't spend it. Training takes time. But it's the best lifelong investment a person can make. Invest time in training."
> — *Jeffrey Gitomer*

7. Your Library Is the Artesian Well of Knowledge.

"What a fine thing your brain is; your brain is a part of all it has met; hence, meet great men -- you can meet them in books."

— How to Close a Sale-*NCR*

"Formal education will earn you a living, self-education will earn you a fortune."

— *Jim Rohn*

"You determine how much of a fortune you want to earn by how much you decide to self-educate."

— *Jeffrey Gitomer*

It's difficult to read books if you don't own them. A library full of success books gives you the opportunity to gain the wisdom of others if you just employ this one word: READ.

If you want to know the intimate thought patterns of someone else, look at their library.

What they read usually determines how they think. If you decide to read about success, the odds are you will become successful. Your library is something to build upon to help you continue your studying.

John D. Rockefeller didn't use a library card. He endowed the library. Reason? He bought books and kept them instead of borrowing them for a week.

Books are not just for reading. They are also for reference.

People often say to me, "I read that book."
People **rarely** say to me, "I use the principles of that book every day." If you own the book, there is a possibility that you might go back and refer to the book for additional knowledge or clarification.

Where is your personal library? What books constitute your library? What books are you using?

Training doesn't get you to the top of your plateau. Education does. Training teaches you how. Education teaches you WHY. Think about reading: Start by reading books about things you love or are interested in. That will begin to create the habit. And the thirst for knowledge. Knowledge, like any other addiction, is a drug. Fifteen beers? Or fifteen books? One will get you to the men's room, the other will allow you to own the men's room. Dedication to lifelong learning means reading and listening to something for your personal development at least an hour a day. Makes sense!

Exercise: List the books you HAVE read that improved your sales game. Now, what book SHOULD you have read to improve your sales game? Ouch! Want the list? **Go to www.gitomer.com and enter MAKE SENSE in the GitBit box.**

More exercise: Read three books at once, a chapter at a time.

More, more exercise: Read two pages a day of a positive-attitude book for the next 25 years.

Note of caution: Old personal development books (Hill, Marden, Carnegie) are hokey. BUT they are equally as valid. Idiots will pass them off as passé and not read them.

Don't be an idiot!

8. Planning Prevents Wandering and Provides Direction.

"If you plan your work, you will not find yourself standing on the corner wondering where to go next."

— *John H. Patterson*

"Goals are the road map that will direct you to success."   — *Jeffrey Gitomer*

The same people who use road maps for traveling often omit road maps for succeeding.

A solid plan of attack for personal development, product knowledge, and market penetration will provide a faster, more successful result.

There's an old cliché that if Moses had had a map, he would not have had to wander for forty years.

Got map?

Post-it Note your way to real achievement.

I have developed the best, easiest method for achieving goals. Go get a pad of Post-it Notes. Put a dozen goals on your bathroom mirror, big goals and small goals. By looking at them every morning and every evening, you will begin to take action. Achievement action. Just a little each day (the daily dose) until one day a goal is achieved.

After you complete the achievement, take it off your bathroom mirror and post it on your bedroom mirror. Every day, as you get dressed, you can see (and relive) your success!

A personal mission statement is your affirmation, philosophy, and purpose rolled into one.

It's an opportunity to bring your goals into focus and transfer your ideals into the real world. It's a chance for you to write your own legacy. It's your personal challenge to yourself. Sounds pretty heavy, but actually it's fun if you do it right.

Do you write down your goals?
How many have you accomplished in the last month or year? What would help you meet your goals in the next 30 days? Six months? Or one year? Don't let your goals fall by the wayside (like your New Year's resolutions).

Exercise:
Direct yourself. Each day, create one single direction that you must achieve. Even if your ass falls off. Just one thing that at the end of each day you can say, "I did it!" After a month, it will be easy to add one more thing. At the end of a year, you will be doing ten things a day and accomplishing them all.

Notice I did not say, "make a long-term plan." I DID say, "take daily actions." If you take the right daily actions, the long-term plans are automatically achieved. Long-term goals can be overwhelming. Short daily directed actions are easily achieved. The secret is the "Daily Dose."

9. Use "Today Time Management."

"Nothing in business is as valuable
as time."

— John H. Patterson

"The successful person takes advantage
of time; the unsuccessful person laments
in the lack of it."

— Jeffrey Gitomer

Every person has the same amount of time.

A wise investment of time is the best nonmonetary investment you can make. Time management is intuitive for some, but it can also be a learned process.

The basic underlying principle of time management is "do what's important first."

Patterson had a "things to do today" chart which hung on the wall in his office. It was very big so there was no way he could avoid it. Patterson wanted to make sure that all tasks, large or small, were completed in the time frame given. If they were, he knew that he had had a productive day. He believed in this time management strategy for his salesmen and for the executives of NCR.

Time management is not complicated -- unless you take a time management course. Then you have to have a minor degree in rocket science to figure out what piece of paper gets what notes in what category and with what priority.

Create Post-it Notes with the day's tasks.
At the end of the day, check them off.
If you didn't accomplish any, you didn't
have a productive day.

Time management is instinctive. You already know what to do. Your problem is not doing it.

Here's the easiest way to think about your time management. If you prioritize A tasks, B tasks, and C tasks, never do a B task until you've done all your A's.

Many people make the mistake of getting the little things out of the way before they tackle the big things.

Get the big things out of the way first, and the little things will disappear.

Exercise: Get in front of people who can say Yes. This is the single highest priority and most productive use of your time. The time you spend face-to-face is in direct proportion to the number of sales you will make.

Want to double your sales?

Easy -- just double the time you spend in front of people who can say **Yes** to you.

Patterson addressing the 100 Point Club, 1912.

"People do not realize the immense
value of utilizing spare minutes."

— *Orison Swett Marden*

"Turn off the TV at home -- it's pretty
much a waste of time. Invest your time
in reading a book."

— *Jeffrey Gitomer*

10. Prospect for Probable Purchasers.

"Take it for granted that everyone can
buy, rather than determining without
an interview that some people will not
buy."   — *John H. Patterson*

"Good fundamental sales skills
and solid product knowledge are
meaningless unless you see and follow-
up the proper number of prospects."

— *Jeffrey Gitomer*

Every prospector was in search of a gold mine. "Gold fever," they called it.
They would pay any amount of money for the map that would lead them
to the gold. Many paid with their lives.

Prospecting for probable purchasers is not as dangerous but is equally
as rewarding.

How to prospect is equally as important as *where* to prospect.

Or better stated, proper prospecting prevents poverty.

Prospecting was and still is an important part of earning the sale.
The NCR salesmen were given a territory and expected to earn a sale
from all businesses in that territory. As each salesman traveled through
a town, they were expected to stop at every local business and call on
every merchant.

However, prospecting was much more difficult in the 1900s because of the lack of technology. Salesmen couldn't Google the company they wanted to call on. They couldn't look up their website. They couldn't send an e-mail to someone in the company. They had to talk to nearby store owners or others in town who might know the probable purchaser they wanted to call on.

As NCR grew, prospecting became easier for the salesmen because of the number of referrals that were made.

Looking for new probable purchasers? Who isn't?

You probably have hundreds you're not paying attention to … YOUR PRESENT CUSTOMERS!

They already know you and like you; you have established rapport, confidence, and trust; you know they have good credit because they have paid you in the past; and you know they will return your call!

I don't think you have to ask for much more than that. Beats cold calling!

With a few exceptions, there is very little difference between one company and another, or one company's products or another's.

The following are the simple (but not easy) personal characteristics of why customers will buy from you. All of which you have probably heard before, but doing them AND believing them AND living them makes the difference!

Here are your personal mantras for finding probable purchasers:

I Work Hard.
"Work only half a day. It makes no difference which half -- the first 12 hours or the last 12 hours."
– Kemmons Wilson

I Bring Solid Value.
Provide something of value that will benefit the PP that your competition cannot match.

I am Responsive.
Try to always exceed your customers' expectations in all contacts you may have with them. Customers want you to get to the point, and they want you to get there fast.

I am a Straight Shooter.
Build a reputation as an honest person. Tell the truth and you don't have to worry about what you say coming back to haunt you.

I Build a Great Reputation.
Do the right things consistently and you will build a reputation that precedes you. Your reputation will make it easier for you to continue to work with your existing customers, and to prospect, new customers. If you have a bad reputation, good luck getting rid of it!

I Listen to Understand.
If you are not so busy doing all of the talking, your customers in most cases will tell you exactly what they want and what you need to do to "get the business."

I Keep My Customers in Front of My Face.
Keep your key customer list on your desk. If you have not spoken with one of them in a while, pick up the phone before your competition does.

I Follow Through.
Say what you will do, and do what you say you will do. Follow-through develops reputation. So do dropped balls.

I Find Their Comfort Zone.
Once you get a customer in a comfort zone, you have to screw up to lose them. Like an old shoe or a favorite shirt, they will be reluctant to seek out alternatives as long as you "feel good." If they look elsewhere, look in the mirror as to why.

The most important reason my customers do business with me: I Still Ask for the Business.
Your customers want to know that they continue to be important, and that you are still hungry.

Exercise:

Call one customer a day and ask for their business. Put down the book and call one NOW!

11. Increase Business Connections to Increase Sales.

"A good plan is to have your agents
assemble … and have each one
explain to you his methods of selling
and the arguments he uses …
a convention of this sort will put
dollars into your pocket."

— *John H. Patterson*

"Networking is creating momentum
toward business and career success."

— *Jeffrey Gitomer*

Today it's called networking.

Patterson was a proponent of business people interacting with one
another. Trade shows, conventions, business meetings, seminars,
and business gatherings of all kinds.

Patterson was able to make sales in any social environment. From
banquets to ballgames. From picnics to presidential retreats. He understood
that business was not simply completed at a sales call or in an office,
and that often his biggest deals were made in nonbusiness environments
or during atypical "business" hours.

Consider the
five basic rules of networking.

1. Go where the probable purchasers are
2. Give first
3. Dig in
4. Be consistent
5. Get to know people on a friendly basis

How well do you do? How would you rate yourself, and more importantly, how would your COMPETITION rate you and rate themselves? Time to get in gear and get out there!

People tend to do business with people they trust.

Be sincere and **be yourself**.

Have breakfast, have dinner, have fun with your PP, and you will build a basic platform upon which they will WANT to do business with YOU.

Exercise:

List five places
where your
five best customers go.
Go there.

12. Creating the Demand Converts Selling to Buying.

"If the prospect understood the proposition, he would not have to be sold; he would come to buy."

— *John H. Patterson*

"People don't like to be sold, but they love to buy."

— *Jeffrey Gitomer*

John Patterson's objective was not to sell cash registers. Rather, **he created the demand for a receipt**.

He encouraged people at every possible moment to "ask for a receipt." This message reached people without cash registers and provoked thought in a manner that produced the desire to purchase his machines.

Desire leads to demand.

At the top of each machine, Patterson put a marketing message. First it was "ask for a receipt." Later it was "amount of purchase," so people could confirm the total on the receipt to the amount displayed on the register.

AMOUNT PURCHASED

THIS REGISTERS THE AMOUNT OF YOUR PURCHASE

NOTICE: MONEY MUST BE REGISTERED BEFORE GOODS ARE WRAPPED

THE COMPANY'S NAME (PERSONALIZED RECEIPT)

GET A RECEIPT

Every customer who walked by an NCR cash register saw a marketing message. The more often people saw the message, the more Patterson's business grew. What message are you sending every time a customer makes a purchase from you?

Create the need. Prove the need. Don't just sell the product.

Why do you buy personal objects? Is it a NEED, or a WANT? Patterson was the first to understand that buying was an emotional process. You must create a balance between the emotion to trigger the sale and the logic to justify the purchase.

You've seen it at Christmas. Cabbage Patch dolls, Tickle Me Elmo stuffed toys. The latest craze. The average consumer can't get enough of it. That's demand. If you could do the same for your business, it would be a much easier life than the one you've got.

Demand comes from desire.
Desire comes from perceived value or gain.

Exercise: List five values (not benefits) that a customer receives by purchasing from you. I'll bet you can't.

13. A Prepared Demonstration Means Personalized!

"Don't go out shooting until you have
your ammunition ready."

— *John H. Patterson*

"A fumbling, excuse-making,
apologizing salesperson builds zero
confidence."

— *Jeffrey Gitomer*

Most salespeople are only halfway prepared to give a sales presentation or sales demonstration.

They know many things about themselves and not enough about how the
PP (probable purchaser) profits from the use of their products.

This is not caused by lack of preparation, this is caused by lack of
proper preparation.

A demonstration must be both personalized -- meaning that it's in terms of the customer's needs, not in terms of what you offer -- and it must be different from and better than your competition.

If your presentation is perceived by the PP as relatively the same as your competition, then all that will matter is your price.

If your presentation combines personalization and differentiation, you can win the sale on value. Differentiation is achieved by being certain that you ask questions and make statements that your competition does not ask or say.

The combination of personalized and differentiation is a formula that will lead to sales. Lots of sales.

NOTE: Failure does not come from lack of sales; failure comes from lack of preparation.

Outcomes are predetermined if you prepare.

Think about it. Isn't it worth the ten minutes it takes to make the sale easy? As they say in Boy Scouts, "If you ain't ready and rehearsed, you won't get the merit badge."

How well do you prepare for your presentation? Do you know more than his or her name, title, and the company name when you walk into the PP's office?

Before your next presentation, have a handle on these five statements:

1. I know who the probable purchaser is currently purchasing my product or service from.

2. I know whether the probable purchaser has sole authority to purchase from us or whether purchasing decisions are a committee decision.

3. I know whether anyone from my company has called on this probable purchaser before.

4. I know whether the probable purchaser ever bought from us before and, if so, why he or she didn't continue to purchase from us.

5. I know how my probable purchaser will profit from his purchase of my product.

Exercise: Learn to employ the rule of 50+50=50 ... Spend 50% of your time preparing ideas and answers about how your customer will benefit. You will give a 50% better presentation, and you will walk away with 50% more business.

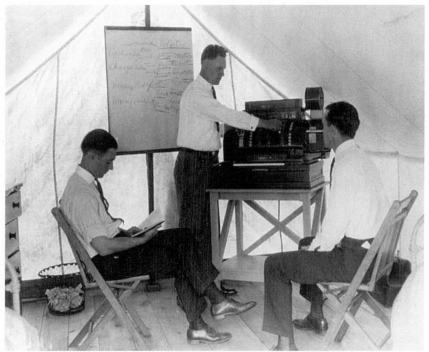

The NCR Archive at the Montgomery Historical Society

Sales agents practicing personalized demonstrations, c1925.

"'Good enough' is the enemy of
all progress."
— *John H. Patterson's favorite quote*

"If you don't personalize your sales
presentation, you will lose to someone
who does."
— *Jeffrey Gitomer*

Hint: Let the probable purchaser do the demo as much as possible.
Tactile involvement leads to a sense of ownership.

14. Gain Interest with Information about the PP not the We-We.

"Always leave him (the merchant) in such a frame of mind that he will be glad to have you call again."

— *John H. Patterson*

"Product knowledge is useless until you know how your product is used on the job to benefit and create profit for the customer."

— *Jeffrey Gitomer*

In order to arouse the interest of a probable purchaser, it is the responsibility of the salesperson to be interesting.

The best way to gain the interest of the PP is to share methods and strategies for profitability and productivity and save the boring (non-interesting) details for later.

Since the cash register wasn't something that everyone thought they needed at first, NCR salesmen had to find a way to gain the attention of a merchant before trying to pitch the sale. Patterson believed in these five steps to get the merchant interested.

Five Steps in Interesting the Merchant (from *The Primer*)

1. Use indirect ways of interesting the merchant.
2. Call on the merchant.
3. Secure necessary information and study the store systems.
4. Get the merchant to realize weak points in his current system.
5. Make a definite appointment.

In my experience, I have found that if a PP wants to know about your product, he or she will ask. In the meantime, you, the salesperson, have a responsibility to gather information directly from the probable purchaser in addition to that which you can get from ordinary means.

For example, don't ask the probable purchaser about anything you could have researched yourself on the Internet. Rather, formulate questions from what you have learned on the Internet to let the PP know you have done your homework. This will make the probable purchaser more eager to talk to you.

If you have taken an interest in them, they will take an interest in you.

How much talking does the PP do when you and he meet? How many PROFIT ideas are you bringing with you?

Remember that the probable purchaser is most interested in HIS benefit from buying your product or service.

Use the "You" method, not the "I" method.

Talk about your probable purchaser's interests rather than your own if you want to keep his attention.

The more you know about them, the easier it is to sell them.
If you bring your knowledge about the PP and how they **profit from use** -- not how they save -- how they profit -- the more likely it is that they will buy from you.

Exercise: Videotape yourself giving a sales presentation. How many we-we phrases are you using? Are you boring your PP with drivel about your company? If someone were giving YOU this presentation, how long would it take for you to fall asleep?

Now count the number of times you specifically address the needs and concerns of the PP. Are you even connecting with them? Take note and take heart -- and change your presentation.

It's got to be all about the PP, not the We-We.

If you walk in with information about you, they consider you a salesman.

If you walk in with ideas and answers, they consider you a resource.

Which one are you?

15. Questions Lead to Answers. Answers Lead to Sales.

"Questions … may start a train of thought that will lead to good results."
— *John H. Patterson*

"Questions are the heart of the sale."
— *Jeffrey Gitomer*

In 1888, Sherlock Holmes stated, "It is a capital offense to theorize before one has data." This was actually said by Holmes on behalf of Arthur Conan Doyle. Preparing the proper questions will lead to answers in which the prospective purchaser will convince himself that he is making the right decision to buy. The proper questions will lead to answers that bind potential profit with probable purchase.

Want to get your PP to think? All you have to do is ask questions. The key to questioning is to get the person to say (or think), "I've never been asked that before." The questions NCR salesmen asked challenged the PP to think about their business and the financial system it currently used. Questions such as, "Do you know exactly how much money was received in the last business day? Do you know exactly how much money went out in the last business day? Do you know that your employees are 100% accurate when opening the cash box and collecting and receiving money?", created the demand for the register and showed the customer the value in owning one. Patterson saw that in the process of selling, questions helped create the demand, let the PP see the value in the product, gave the salesman input about the PP's business and needs, and helped him close the sale. Any questions?

What can the proper power questions do for you? Engage the probable purchaser and earn more sales!

Do you have 25 of them -- the most powerful questions you can create -- at your fingertips?

No? Join the crowd. 95% of all salespeople don't. That could be why only 5% of salespeople rise to the top. Just a theory (or is it?).

Here are the 7.5 questioning success strategies:

1. Ask the probable purchaser questions that make him evaluate new information.

2. Ask questions that qualify needs.

3. Ask questions about improved productivity, profits, or savings.

4. Ask questions about company or personal goals.

5. Ask questions that separate you from your competition -- not compare you to them.

6. Ask questions that make the customer or probable purchaser think before giving a response.

7. Ask Power Questions to create a BUYING atmosphere -- not a selling one.

7.5 A critical success strategy: To enhance your listening skills, write down answers. It proves you care, preserves your data for follow-up, keeps the record straight, and makes the customer feel **important**.

Exercise: Ask the wrong questions, get the wrong answers. Here's the challenge: Get one probable purchaser or customer to say, "No one ever asked me that before."

16. Listening Leads to Understanding.

"Don't talk for the sake of talking."
— *John H. Patterson*

"Listening is one of the most important aspects of the selling process, yet it's usually the weakest part of a sales professional's skill set."
— *Jeffrey Gitomer*

There are two basic kinds of listening: listening with the intent to respond and listening with the intent to understand.

Listening with intent to respond leads to interruption. This lesson focuses on the science of using both disciplines in the order of understanding FIRST, and responding SECOND.

Here's a two-word lesson on listening -- it's the only/best way to be certain your listening skills are as good as your selling skills. And those two words are not "Shut up!" The two words are: **Take notes.**

Note-taking makes listening a certainty, and lets the customer know his words are valuable enough to write down.

Are you a talker or a listener? Learn to be as good at shutting up as you are at talking.

When you leave a meeting, does your recollection of it ever differ from the person who was sitting right next to you? Maybe it's because you were distracted -- most likely it's because you didn't take notes.

Ever catch yourself formulating the next words to come out of your mouth rather than listening to the person until they were done speaking? Sure you have -- it's human nature. Don't do that.

Here's a method toward error-free positive communication ...

1. Focus eye contact on the communicator.

2. Write the communication down.

3. Repeat it back or ask about it.

4. Get confirmation.

4.5 Deliver what you promised.

Exercise: LEARN how to be a better listener by asking a question at the end of their statement. If you make a statement, it's possible that you were interrupting. But with a question, you almost HAVE to wait until they're finished speaking.

17. Less Sell-Talk Time Leads to More Buy-Time.

"Don't talk all the time. Give the merchant a chance."

— *John H. Patterson*

"If you listen better, you will sell more."

— *Jeffrey Gitomer*

The balance between letting the PP talk and the salesman talk must be weighed heavily in favor of the PP. Most salespeople make the fatal mistake of selling when in fact the more the PP talks, the more they will sell themselves on the product or service.

The salesman's responsibility is to create ways to let the PP have more talk time. This is done through powerful questioning. The more powerful the question, the more "probable purchaser" becomes "profitable customer."

Salespeople think they have to "sell" to make the sale, and nothing could be further from the truth. If you let the customer talk long enough, they will see the purpose and value of saying yes. They will sell themselves.

Questions and listening go hand in hand.

The only person who loses by having poor listening skills is you! How are you listening? Do you know how and when to be quiet? You can learn a lot from your PP if you give them the chance to talk!

Look for these two symptoms of lousy listeners:

A person who seems to have all the answers usually isn't listening.

A person who interrupts isn't listening (or at least is not a good listener).

Exercise: Ask every customer a two-part question that when answered would be a reason to buy. First ask what their experience has been. Let them talk. Then ask why they are buying now, and what they hope to gain as a result of purchase.

This exercise will give the PP maximum talk time -- and give you maximum understanding of their situation.

18. Your Message Must Be as Compelling as Your Product to Engage the PP.

"You interest people, first, by the thing you talk about; and second, by the way you talk."

— *Manual for NCR Salesmen*

"The secret to sales is not just engagement, it is *INTELLIGENT* engagement."

— *Jeffrey Gitomer*

The key to any sale rests in how well you engage the probable purchaser.

If you engage the probable purchaser, you create an atmosphere to buy. If you not only engage at the beginning, but also at the end of the meeting, the probable purchaser is eager to buy.

Your preparation, the questions you ask, the ideas you bring, your communication and presentation skills, and your positive attitude and enthusiasm are the keys to intelligent engagement.

The old adage is, "It's not what you say -- it's how you say it." Wrong. In sales it's *both*. Making a great sales presentation is a marriage of "what you say" and "how you say it."

The list below concentrates on *how you say it*. If you deliver the greatest sales pitch in the world with no enthusiasm, sincerity, or belief -- you'll lose the sale.

In the beginning of a sales presentation, there are 4.5 elements that determine whether a sale will be made or not.

1. Rapport -- Putting yourself on the same side of the fence with the probable purchaser.

2. Need -- Determining what the probable purchaser deems as the factors that will influence his motivation to listen with the intent to purchase.

3. Importance -- The weight that a probable purchaser assigns to a product, feature, benefit, price, or time frame.

4. Confidence -- Your ability to gain credibility. Your ability to remove all doubt. Your ability to gain comfort that the risk of purchase will be less than the reward of ownership.

4.5 Value Transferred -- Your ability to get the probable purchaser to perceive that he gains the most value by buying your product or service, AND you are the most valuable person to buy it from.

While all of the information from these elements can be acquired by asking the right power questions, *the difference between good and great salespeople is the way they present (deliver) their message.*

Much is said about sales techniques to coerce or persuade the probable purchaser to buy. Not much is said (or written) about sales presentation skills -- fundamental communication competence, combined with public speaking adeptness to blend a symphonic (sales) pitch.

Your speaking skills must be used throughout the entire presentation, but they're critical at the start, because they create an impression and set a tone for the rest of the meeting.

An engaging question is one that makes the person stop and think, and respond in terms of you.

What is the most engaging question in the world?...
Will You Marry Me?

Will you marry me? is a question about the PP, that makes them stop and think, and respond in terms of you. What is your "Will you marry me" question? Do you have one? How much of a commitment do your PPs make when they answer your questions?

Real engagement is the most difficult part of selling because the salesperson (you) is unprepared to engage. Oh, you may be prepared to sell -- (insert crap about you and your product) -- but you are ill-prepared to engage (stuff about the customer and how he profits from purchase). Create five great engagement questions.

No two sales presentations are alike. Even if you're selling the same product and work for the same company.

Making a presentation is complex even if you're selling paper clips. Making a presentation is delicate, even if you're selling 18-wheel trucks. Everyone has a different style of selling -- BUT the elements of content and process in a presentation must be the same. You master the elements, then adapt them to your style. It's what you say (the elements) combined with how you say it (your style). Here are the 10.5 ways to prepare for your sales presentation so you can be sure to win the sale:

1. Get ready -- the content, the humor, the speed of delivery, the tone, the gesture, the passion, the familiarity, the story, the conciseness, the punch. (Clue: Know the audience, pre-question some of the attendees, or die.)

2. Ask yourself eight questions ...

>   **A.** What's my time limit?
>
>   **B.** Is this the most compelling message I can create?
>
>   **C.** What's the point? What will compel me to act?
>
>   **D.** Am I clear, is my message clear?
>
>   **E.** Is my delivery the best it can be?
>
>   **F.** Would I buy?
>
>   **G.** What do I want the audience to do when I'm done?
>
>   **H.** What do I want them to say to me (about me) when it's over?

3. Practice in front of people not afraid to criticize you.

4. Audiotape a practice session. If you listen to the audio and say to yourself, "That sucks," that's what the audience will hear. That's you -- fix it.

5. Listen to your tape as often as you can stand it. Memorize and know where you need emphasis. Know what sounds stupid -- cut that out.

6. Practice it as though you were giving it. Rehearse for real every time.

7. If your family or friends think you're nuts -- you're on the right track.

8. Get an evaluator before you start each talk.

9. Videotape the actual session.

10. Watch the tape twice. Make a list of "never do that again" and carry it with you for three years.

10.5 Join Toastmasters.

Go to www.toastmasters.org and find the closest Toastmasters to you ... and register while you are there!

 Exercise: Substitute television with sales-call preparation. Give up TV for two nights a week, and just prepare questions that will engage the probable purchaser, gather valuable information, and ask for the sale. I promise you it will put more money in your pocket than watching your favorite show.

19. An Objection Is the Gateway to a Sale.

"An objection is nearly always
an advantage to the salesman ...
to turn the objection into a real
reason for buying."

— John H. Patterson

"The sale starts when the customer
objects."   *— Jeffrey Gitomer*

The training manual *Selling Helps for NCR Salesmen* prepared all of
Patterson's men with answers to any objection they might encounter.
Patterson saw objections as windows to more sales, and he was right. If a
merchant objected to price, quality, service, or anything else, it was at this
moment the salesman would qualify the product, show the value, and at
the same time, create confidence in the buyer. The NCR salesmen were
prepared for objections. Are you? Each salesman knew exactly how to
respond to every doubt in the merchant's mind. Maybe that's why the
company is still around 120 years later. How many sales are you losing
because you aren't prepared to overcome objections? Answer: Too many.

When a PP objects, protests, rejects, or denies, he is giving a signal that he
does not believe in or trust in you, the product, or the company and that
more information is needed. If you become deflated when you hear an
objection, it is likely you may not make many sales. This is a curable
condition once you understand the PP's cues.

Objections actually indicate interest and the need
for more clarification or more proof on the part
of the PP, and the salesperson's responsibility
is to provide it enthusiastically.

Look forward to objections.
They are the gateway to a sale.

If you can overcome an objection in your presentation before the probable purchaser raises it, you are more likely to make a sale.

Major clue ...
an objection may actually indicate purchaser interest!

6.5 steps to identify the true objection and learn how to overcome it:

1. Listen to the objection and decide if it's true.

2. Qualify it as the only one.

3. Confirm it again in a different way.

4. Qualify the objection to set up the close.

5. Answer the objection so that it completely resolves the issue and confirms the resolve.

6. Ask a closing question or communicate to the PP in an assumptive (I have the sale in hand) manner.

6.5 Confirm the answer and the sale in writing.

Exercise: Create five answers for the PP's biggest objections. You know they're coming, why not be ready to answer them in a creative way?

20. Selling Is Not Manipulating; Selling Is Harmonizing.

"The successful salesman must learn to be all things to all people."
— *John H. Patterson*

"Understand how your product is used (not just what it does) so you can understand how to harmonize with your prospect and sell it most effectively."
— *Jeffrey Gitomer*

Selling is about understanding the other person. Each person has different motives to buy based on personality and needs. Salesmen cannot give the same presentation all the time. You've got to adapt the presentation to meet the needs and the personality of the PP. Patterson changed the register models presented to fit the PPs' personality type, not just their business type. This innovation made the product seem custom-fit for the purchaser.

I'm against systems of selling. They teach you a way. Usually a manipulative way. And you gotta use that way. The problem is the probable purchaser may not want to buy that way. Which way do you sell?

Harmony is understanding, sensing the tone and comfort level of the PP.

As a SalesMaster, your job is to take the characteristics of the probable purchaser and blend them with the reason the PP is buying so that it motivates the PP to act. And gives the PP enough confidence to buy.

Think of harmony in music. Think of it the same way in sales.

Are you in sync with your PP? Are you in-tune or off-key?

Here are a few guidelines that will work on any type of purchaser:

1. Never argue.

2. Never offend.

3. Never think or act like you are defeated.

4. Try to make a friend at all costs.

5. Try to get on the same side of the fence (harmonize).

5.5 Never have to remember what you said. (A. Write it down. B. Don't lie.)

Exercise: Write down the last five conflicts you had with a PP during a sale. Write down how you could have avoided them.

Try them the next time the same conflict situation arises.

21. Complete the Sale with an Agreement to Buy ... and Be Certain to Give Them a Receipt.

"Closing the sale is getting the probable purchaser's decision to buy."
— *John H. Patterson*

"Assume the sale."
— *Jeffrey Gitomer*

Most salespeople are willing to walk away from a sales situation without an answer regarding the PP's intent to purchase. The true PP will have no objection to being asked to purchase. Many times a salesperson is in the middle of a selling cycle and even here the sale must be asked for. You must always ask to confirm the next step in the cycle of selling. Refer to it as the principle of "one YES leads to another."

Patterson had it right.
It's not "closing" the sale,
it's "completing" the sale.
Huge difference.
Closing is pushing.
Completing is the last step
in the process of buying.

How do you complete the sale?
What is your selling cycle time?
What could you do to make it shorter?

Do that! How many meetings/presentations/phone calls does it take you to close the sale? And remember, you are a SALESperson and the PP is EXPECTING you to ask for the sale. Don't disappoint him.

5.5 closing strategies and tactics that you will find effective:

1. Challenge the probable purchaser to do what's best for his business -- This strategy is great when the PP is doing business with an existing vendor or friend, and they are not providing the best product or service.

2. We are experts at what we do -- And you can have peace of mind to do what you do best, knowing our part of your job will get done. Always let the PP have a path to doing what they do best, and have peace of mind that your service will supplement that process on their way to success.

3. Make a list of objectives for what the PP wants to accomplish AFTER your product or service is in place -- Your objective as a professional is to get the PP to see the world as though the sale were already made.

4. Get the PP to be a visionary -- Let the PP tell you what he has in mind, instead of you telling him what's on yours.

5. Make the PP commit to a future action -- This strategy must be worded more out of conversation than sales presentation so it doesn't sound *too salesy*.

5.5 Make plans for after the sale has taken place, before the sale is consummated -- Even if you don't have the commitment yet, you can try to schedule an installation time, or a meeting after delivery.

Exercise: Start by looking at your last five sales. How did they happen? How did you complete them? Now make a plan to incorporate those strategies into every presentation and every sales cycle.

Success in sales is repeatable, if you learn from your successes.

22. Service is the Reputation for the Next Sale.

"Quality in selling starts with service."

— John H. Patterson

"Your friendliness and willingness
to help is in direct proportion to
your success."

— Jeffrey Gitomer

"To serve is to rule" is a 5,000-year-old Chinese proverb. The more a salesperson learns that service is the biggest part of the sale, the more his reputation will grow as an honest, ethical, helpful, and sincere businessperson worthy of repeat business and a referral.

All customers need service. The big question is: **How do you respond?**

Here are the five divisions of service that the NCR salesman delivered in each sale (listed in *The Primer*). How do you compare?

1. Service before selling (finding out general problems in the business now)
2. Service in selling (selling the proper machine to the merchant)
3. Installation service (install the machine properly and educate the merchant as to how each feature operates)
4. Follow-up service (call back to find out any problems or answer any questions)
5. Organization service (giving efficient repair service and supplies)

Each salesman had to deliver service before, during, and after the presentation and after the sale.

"Serve your merchants and they will in
turn serve you."

— John H. Patterson

Why do some of your customers
love you and some hate you?

Why do some stay loyal and some leave?

What can you do to make
your service memorable?

What are you doing to maintain
real customer loyalty?

Loyal is the most difficult of the customer service goals to achieve. But once you have it, you have something your competition will never have -- the next order. Give solutions, not excuses. That is what customers want.

Exercise: Call five customers at random, and ask them how they feel about doing business with you. Ask them why they would do business with you again.

Then call your five best customers, and ask them why they will do business with you again. Then call five customers you lost and find out why you lost them.

Those twenty answers, when combined and studied, will give you the answers you need to grow and prosper with a combination of new customers, and well-retained old customers.

23. Extra Service Leads to the "Testimonial Word."

"Give them that little extra service
which keeps customers pleased …
remember, a satisfied user is the best
advertisement you can have."

— *John H. Patterson*

"Exceptional service lowers the barriers
to testimonial sales."

— *Jeffrey Gitomer*

All customers expect great service. Very few get it. What happens from the
time the sale is made until the next purchase is about to be made determines
who gets the next order. The "service" part of the relationship you have with
your customers determines your fate for future business.

Your biggest job is not to sell. Your biggest job is to deliver MEMORABLE service.

Going beyond what is expected means surprising, anticipating, delighting,
and even rescuing the customer at a precise moment in time. Consistently
going beyond what is expected leads to stories and referrals. It's also
known as word-of-mouth advertising.

Your customers can be walking, talking testimonials.

When you are done speaking with a customer or the transaction is over, that
is when they START talking. They will say one of three things … something
good, nothing, or something bad … and the cool part is you choose by the
way you act around them, and the way you treat them. How are you
treating your customers? What are your customers saying about you?

Facts and figures are forgotten but stories are retold again and again. Exceptional service lowers the barrier to testimonial sales. If you have created exceptional opportunities for your customer, they will be more than happy to tell their story to the media and to other prospective customers.

You don't need permission from a boss to make a customer feel great.

Think about a time when you felt good because you had good service. Make someone else feel that good feeling.

Pick out one customer every day and make them feel great!

Here are your possibilities as you look at the service process: Your customer *MAY* come back if the product was good and the service was acceptable (this is satisfied). Your customer *WILL* come back if the product was great (this is loyal). Your customer *WILL COME BACK **AND TELL OTHERS*** if the product was the greatest, and the service was memorable (that is the definition of loyal, testimonial, and referral).

Exercise: Look at your last five referrals. How did they come about? Measure how many unsolicited referrals you get each week. Five should be a minimum number. Then create a game plan of what you can do EVERY DAY that the customer would consider memorable, and do that.

Customer service is not about who's right or wrong. It's about how you react to, respond, and handle the problem.

24. Referrals Are Better Earned than Asked for.

"Satisfied users are always your best advertisement, and the more of them you have in your territory the more money you will make."

— *John H. Patterson*

"A referral is the easiest sale to make."

— *Jeffrey Gitomer*

There are two basic types of referrals. Solicited and unsolicited. A solicited referral is one that you ask for. Unsolicited referrals are the ones that you earn. There are two basic forms of unsolicited referrals: customer-driven and PP-driven. Unsolicited referrals are like a business report card -- it will tell you how well you are performing in the marketplace. You will ONLY get an unsolicited referral when you are at the highest level of market performance.

If you have a happy customer, you can earn a referral. But earning referrals requires extra work. Service is the key. Excellent service provided by you, along with the excellent service provided by your company, is the best formula to gain and earn referrals. If you make 100 cold calls, how many sales will you make? If you get 100 referrals, how many sales will you make? Get it? The highest percentage sale is a referral.

The definition of referral is **risk**.

The definition of a referral is risk because someone is willing to risk their friendship or relationship with another to have them contact you for a purchase. People are only willing to risk when they are confident and comfortable that the risk is low and the possible rewards are so high that they outweigh any hesitancy in giving the referral.

Are you willing to refer your clients or customers to someone else? Is someone else willing to refer their clients or customers to you? Answer: Yes, if there is mutual trust.

You could double your business if you got every one of your present customers to refer ONE more customer just like themselves.

If you can't call, or have a hard time calling on your present customer, or if you come up with some lame excuse like, "I've sold them everything I can sell them," it really means:
— You have failed to establish enough rapport with the customer.
— You have probably not followed up well (or at all) after the sale.
— Your customer had some problem, and you are reluctant to call and open a can of worms.
— You are in need of more training.
— And the big one…you have not developed a proper relationship with the customer.

I am constantly amazed at the salespeople who make sales and move to the next prospect.

I challenge you to look at your customer list carefully and honestly. I'll bet there are hundreds of opportunities to sell **something**.

Exercise: List your five biggest customers. List your five best customers (relationship-wise). Are they the same? They better be or you're in trouble. If not, stop here and develop a game plan to make that happen within one year.

More exercise: List five ways you can earn a referral.

More, more exercise: Make a game plan to implement each referral strategy.

25. Testimonials Will Sell When the Salesman Can't.

"Overcome objections with testimonials."
— *John H. Patterson*

"One testimonial has more strength
than a hundred presentations."
— *Jeffrey Gitomer*

When a salesperson speaks of himself, his company, or his product, he is either selling or bragging or both. When a loyal customer speaks on behalf of the product in the form of a testimonial, it is proof, and in fact, it is the only proof that a salesperson has to substantiate his claims. If a customer is on the fence and is choosing between one company and another, it is the testimonial, not the salesperson, which will sway the decision.

Testimonials, like referrals, are report cards. If you are having trouble getting them, that's not a problem … that's a symptom. And you better look deeper into your method of doing business or your product's capability to find the answer. Most salespeople mistakenly blame the customer when they can't get a referral or testimonial. Big mistake.

Testimonials are PROOF -- and they're the only proof you've got.

When is the right time to ask for a testimonial?

Not sure? That might be the reason you don't have as many as you would like. You may be asking at the wrong time or asking the wrong people.

Do you have a notebook full of testimonial letters categorized by topic to show your PP? Don't lay them all out at once -- be sure to pull the right one at the right time, or else it won't work! You must pull the right testimonials that pertain specifically to their objections. Isn't it about time to put your testimonials into 21st-century technology? Isn't a video more powerful than a letter?

Exercise: Select your five BEST customers. The ones who really love you. Make an appointment to see them for a testimonial. A VIDEO testimonial. Live recordings of what they think of you.

If you only do ONE THING from the entire book, do this.

A collection of video testimonials will go further than any other sales tool times ten.

Do a video testimonial CD, and the world is your sales oyster.
If you just use letters, you're just like every other clam.

26. Advertising Brings Awareness. Testimonial Advertising Brings Customers.

"A satisfied user is the best advertisement you could have."
— *John H. Patterson*

"Word-of-mouth advertising is fifty times more powerful than advertising."
— *Jeffrey Gitomer*

Everyone wants to be well known. Everyone wants to be a household word. Everyone wants to be perceived as a leader. And everyone makes the mistake of tooting their own horn in an ad. One third-party endorsement is worth a hundred self-praising ads.

Patterson used several forms of advertising. He tried everything from sending out a circular to 5,000 prospects to creating enticing window displays at his stores that would lure probable purchasers in.

But the most effective form of advertising he found was the use of testimonials. Once he realized that satisfied users were the best advertisement, he encouraged all his salesmen to advertise themselves by becoming identified with the people who were in a position to help them, their loyal customers.

"My registers have saved me the expense of two clerks and increased my volume about 30%."
Cleveland, Tenn.

"Approximately 24% increase in our grocery department sales. At the same time, we have been able to reduce payroll expense in this department approximately 10%."
Pittsburgh, Pa.

"Had a direct saving of $1,820.00 per year in clerk hire alone. Charge business increased immediately."
Dallas, Texas

"Could not possibly handle my present volume without it."
Indianapolis, Ind.

"This system gives us the lowest operating cost we have yet had the pleasure to enjoy."
New York City

"As a result of our change to self-service, volume in store increased more than 60%."
Burlington, Iowa

"Of all the equipment we have placed in our stores during our years of business, none has given us such a great return on our investment as these registers."
Johnson City, Tenn.

"Had I not hesitated so long to avail myself of the advantages your registers offer, I would have been many thousands of dollars better off today."
Redwood City, Calif.

"Since changing to self-service, our volume has increased with same employees, thus reducing expense percentage ... we now handle both cash and charge business with greater ease and efficiency."
Oak Park, Ill.

"After changing to self-service, our sales volume showed a large increase without increasing expenses ... we now have control over departments, cash and charge sales, and tax collections."
St. Louis, Mo.

BEFORE

"Self-service increased our sales over 300% first year. Kept overhead down. Profit greater than we expected it could be. We do both cash and charge business."
Spokane, Wash.

AFTER

you too can enjoy similar benefits..

The NCR Archive at the Montgomery Historical Society

Testimonial ad that appeared May 21, 1947.

"Testimonials are proof that your claims are true."

— *John H. Patterson*

"Customers are the most powerful salespeople on your team."

— *Jeffrey Gitomer*

Testimonials are sales power.

A testimonial ad creates 4.5 winning situations.

1. It provides proof that your product is what you say it is.

2. It strengthens the loyalty bond between you and the customer in the ad.

3. It's the only proof you've got.

4. It reduces the risk of purchasing.

4.5 It deflates the competition (especially if it is a testimonial of a customer who switched).

Who are your five best customers?

How did they choose you?

Did they switch from a competitor?

Do they find value in your services beyond your price?

Will they do a testimonial for you?

If you can create an army of people talking about you, instead of a bunch of self-righteous drivel about "we're the greatest," you'll make more sales than you ever dreamed. The question is, do you have an army of people who love you enough to spread the word?

Exercise: Create a video testimonial for every aspect of your selling process. Work them into your sales presentation at the appropriate times. Watch your sales increase.

Testimonials are more powerful than salespeople.

27. Competition Means Prepare to Be Your Best.

"Treat competition fairly."

— John H. Patterson

"Competition does not mean war.
It means learn, it means prepare,
and it means be your best."

— Jeffrey Gitomer

Competitors want the business just as much as you do. They will fight, they will undercut, they will play dirty, and they will go to any length to prevent you from getting the sale. Your job is to get the sale and maintain your highest standard of doing business. This can be accomplished by out-thinking and out-performing the competition. And you have thousands of people who will help you at any moment in time. You know them … they are your own loyal customers.

Here are two ways to address the competition:

1. Go "over" the competition.
The ideal way to win. It assumes that you take the high ground. It doesn't mean sit back and wait. It means rise above in such a way that the competition has to respond or lose. Here are a few "over" ways: E-zines. Seminars. Referrals. Building value by building profit. Earning testimonials and using them to get "over" again.

More "over." Others speaking on your behalf is better than any sales pitch "against" someone else. I'll make you one promise: If you invest the time and effort it takes to go "over" the competition, you will be rewarded beyond your wildest dreams, AND sales will be easier and more fun.

And once you reach a high level of "**over**" you will be qualified for the highest level …

2. Ignore the competition.

I have spent the last ten years ignoring the competition. Building my presentation skills and writing skills. Competitors read my weekly article in their hometown. They hate me, and I love it.

Do I know them? Some. Most I don't. Sales and competition share the same adage. "It's not who you know, it's who knows you." Sounds a bit stuffy, but let me assure you that it's better to build your skills than to try to "beat" someone.

I go for "best," not "beat." It's a better, cleaner win. Do I always win? No. But I always feel I should have. And I have a self-confidence that keeps me ready for the next opportunity. I wake up the next day and go to work sharpening my skills.

My ways of dealing with my competition (over or ignore) are the hardest ways – but they work. And the longer you go "over" them, the more you can ignore them.

Yes, I want to beat the crap out of the competition -- it's instinctive. But a smarter path is to have them looking over their shoulders to see where you are. Let them "hear your footsteps" and beat them by being "chosen" or "preferred."

How many ways are there to deal with the competition?

How do you deal with them?
What do you say about them?
How do you beat them?
How often do you beat them?

The goal is to separate yourself from the competition and from everyone else.

Have creative, new ideas; have the sale in finished form (design done, preliminary layout, sample); have a WOW multimedia presentation; have a comparison chart of key areas where you beat the competition.

Got boring business cards? Get new ones made, even if it's out of your own pocket.

IMPORTANT NOTE: Don't down the competition. If you have nothing nice to say, say nothing. This is a tempting rule to break ... the sirens are sweetly singing. Set yourself apart from them with preparation and creativity. Don't slam them. Downing the competition is not a no-win situation; it's an absolute losing situation.

When a prospect picks you over the competition, it's a day to celebrate -- and a day to discover "why" -- when you figure out why you were chosen, all you have to do is repeat the process.

Do things (professionally) no one else would do.

Exercise: Look at your last five sales where you were chosen over the competition. Write down the primary factors of why you won.

Do the same thing for losses. Look at your last five sales that you LOST to the competition. Write down the primary factors of WHY you lost.

Now all you have to do is strengthen the reasons why you were chosen and fix the reasons you weren't and ...

PRESTO!
More sales --
and you can
thank the
competition
for them.

Cool.

28. Recognize and Thank Those Who Have Helped You Succeed.

"People seldom improve themselves when they have no other model but themselves to look after."

— *John H. Patterson*

"The game of selling is a TEAM sport, not an individual sport."

— *Jeffrey Gitomer*

"I'd like to thank the members of the academy ..." Don't forget to say thank you to those who helped you along the way. This is true not only if you are a salesperson, this is true for the corporate executives who still have their own washroom and private cafeteria.

Patterson did a tremendous job thanking not only his sales team but ALL of his employees. From rewards through the still-existing "100 Point Club" to factory improvements, rewards, and incentives, Patterson did his best to reward and satisfy each salesman's need for appreciation.

You need co-workers to help you succeed. All at different levels of career achievement. The boss can help you, and so can the truck driver. And most times the lower-level people are the most help. Acknowledge them. Thank them. Reward them. Let them know you care and are grateful for their help.

The Universal Thank You ...
Notice that you will always see
the words **"Thank You!"** on each and
every receipt you are given.

You didn't become a success on your own. And it didn't happen overnight. You may have even been lucky enough to have a mentor.

Take the time to acknowledge the people who have helped you succeed. Some will be readily apparent, but others may have seemed to have been against you when they were just trying to help you help yourself. Learn to discern the difference and thank them ALL.

Exercise: List five people you want to thank or acknowledge. Get a small gift of remembrance for them. I give autographed books. Go to www.executivebooks.com and buy the set of books by Charlie "Tremendous" Jones. If you request autographed copies, he will sign them all at no additional cost. I keep a dozen for gifts.

Oh, and thank **you** for being my customer.

Bonus exercise: Become a mentor to someone who can benefit from your experience and will appreciate your gift of wisdom. Having a mentor is a gift, and can make a world of difference to the person you've invested in. Pass it on.

29. To Get Loyalty, You Must GIVE Loyalty.

"If it's only money you get out of your job, you don't get enough."

— *John H. Patterson*

"Customer loyalty is the highest level of business achievement."

— *Jeffrey Gitomer*

Patterson wrote: "Believe in your goods. Be loyal to your Company. Put your heart in your work." He wrote those words in 1889.

Gitomer's four pillars of loyalty are:

I. Loyalty to your company

II. Loyalty to your product

III. Loyalty to your customer

IV. Loyalty to yourself

Patterson's words and the four pillars of loyalty are the foundation for building long-term business success.

Loyalty is misunderstood. My definition is, will the customer do business with me again, and will the customer refer me to other probable purchasers? If I am loyal to my customers, they will be loyal to me. If I refer other customers to my customers, I am giving them my loyalty, thereby earning theirs. If I set the example by doing for my customers what I want done to me, I will receive what I want by virtue of earning it rather than expecting it or asking for it. Earning is the most powerful way of gaining anything. The easiest loyalty lessons are the ones you learn at home, either by positive or negative example.

Foundations of all buildings and houses start with pillars. Without the proper foundation, you have an unstable building, and an unstable customer.

It is the same in sales. If you don't have the four pillars of loyalty, your sales foundation is shaky.

You must have the loyalty to all four parts.
Loyalty is the highest mark.
Loyalty is success.
Loyalty is solid gold.
Loyalty is golden business.
Loyal is unyielding, unrelenting and ever faithful. True to the end.
And your golden opportunity to win by earning it from others.

So, how do you get to "loyal" in the relationships with your customers? Simple -- apply the principles that build loyalty in every other aspect of your life. Well, sort of simple. Loyalty is more delicate with customers because there is a balance of money and value. And loyalty is not just granted -- it's an earned distinction.

Exercise: List your five MOST loyal customers. Now list the reasons each one is loyal to you. Make a plan to instill those reasons in every one of your customers.

The only measure of loyal customers:
Will they do business with me again?
Will they refer someone else to me?

30. Decide…
It Doesn't Matter If
It's Right or Wrong…
Decide!

"An executive is a man who decides.
Sometimes he decides right. But he
always decides."
— *John H. Patterson*

"If you want to succeed, you have to
fail a few times."
— *Max Gitomer (father)*

This was Patterson's way of saying "Take a risk, take a chance."
Patterson's whole life was risk and chance. He made decisions that
risked his last dime.

Patterson didn't
take risks,
he took
calculated risks.

Patterson himself was a decision maker and he demanded the same from
his executives. He could tolerate employees who made mistakes, but had
no patience with men who feared or hesitated to make a decision.

Decision making came quite easy to Patterson for the simple fact that he had the instinctive and inveterate habit of analyzing situations realistically instead of nominally.

Patterson would reach a decision, no matter how important or menial, by using his famous pyramid chart.

Patterson even went as far as standardizing this chart for his sales team.

The objective needing to be reached (the decision) would be at the apex of the pyramid. Then he added a realistic analysis of the means by which the objective might be attained.

He standardized this method of decision making throughout the organization so it became habitual for all employees in the company to use when a decision needed to be reached.

Patterson wanted all his men to think alike, or at least like him. The pyramid chart was the visual symbol of this. (See a pyramid chart in the hand of Patterson himself on the next page.)

This pyramid chart was drawn by Patterson on the
back page of a book on longevity. Patterson was
inspired by reading, and took immediate action to
write down ideas, concepts, and thoughts.

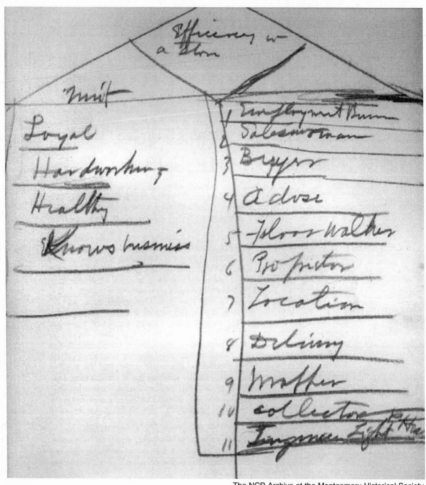

The NCR Archive at the Montgomery Historical Society

Pyramid chart in the hand of John Patterson.

"It's not a matter of 'can't' decide.
It's a matter of 'won't' decide.
Can't means won't."

— *Jeffrey Gitomer*

Think about the last few decisions you delayed.

Why did you? Uncertainty? Timing not "right"? Not wanting to take the risk? You can always change the direction you are going, but not if you are standing still.

Postponing a decision comes from lack of information.
Postponing a decision comes from a lack of factual information to make a sound judgment. Postponing decision comes from confusion or disorganization. Postponing a decision comes from doubt or fear.

NOTE: Monday-morning quarterbacks are the best non-decision makers in the world. They look at someone who took a risk, decided incorrectly, and now here they come saying, "Well, that's not what I would have done!" As they sit with their beer on their chicken's nest, yelling at the TV.

How do you come to decisions?
Is it systematic? Or feeling?
Can't make decisions?
Try to use Patterson's way ...
the Pyramid Chart.

Exercise: Make a pyramid chart for yourself. Start with a decision you'll have to make soon. Refer to the Patterson definitions and examples. Often when you write out the possibilities, the right decision becomes obvious.

31. You Become Known by the Actions You Take. Take Ethical Actions.

"There was a time when all successful salesmen were liars. That time has passed."
　　　　　　　　　— *John H. Patterson*

"You are more known for your deeds and your actions than for your words."
　　　　　　　　　— *Jeffrey Gitomer*

What is ethical? Who decides?

Use the five-question acid test during the presentation ...

1. Is this in the best long-term interest of the customer?

2. Is this in the best long-term interest of my company?

3. Is this in the best long-term interest of my career?

4. If I were the probable purchaser, would I buy?

5. Is it something that would make my mother proud?

These five questions are at the heart of ethics in the selling process. They must be asked every time a sale is being proposed.

Patterson knew 100 years ago the importance of ethics in business, and wanted his men to portray a trusting, pleasing, and earnest image.

My experience has shown me that if you have to say what you are, you probably aren't.

Think about that for a moment. "I'm honest," "I'm ethical," -- even "I'm the decision-maker," "I'm the boss," or "I'm in charge," usually indicates just the opposite. Doesn't it?

There's an easy way to measure the results of your ethics ...

- Can you sell the same customer again?

- Has the customer referred you another customer -- without being asked to do so? Get proof of your ethics, get better, or get out.

- Remember the movie *Pinocchio*? And Jiminy Cricket on the shoulder of Pinocchio? His thought-provoking song, "Always Let Your Conscience Be Your Guide," (and you can probably sing the chorus right now) was a statement of shunning bad ethics. Didn't you already know what he was going to say? And don't you already know what to do? You don't need to ask yourself about ethics. You simply need to take ethical actions from what you already know. If you have any questions, call your mother.

Exercise: The challenge is for you to rededicate yourself to helping or to satisfying the needs of the customer or prospect each time you sell. Your words and actions must be in harmony with the prospect's thoughts and perceptions in order to establish a comfort level that motivates the prospect to buy.

How do you achieve PP comfort level?
You have to believe in it, you have to practice it,
and you have to show your beliefs with deeds
and ethical actions -- every day.

32. If You Have Done Your Homework and Prepared Well, It Will Be Evident in Your Sales Report Card.

"Remember, the demonstration has but one object, the sale of the register. No matter how well you think you have demonstrated the register, if you do not close the sale, you have failed in your purpose."

— *John H. Patterson*

"Weak salespeople look at quotas and become fearful. Mediocre salespeople look at quotas as a goal. Great salespeople look at quotas and laugh."

— *Jeffrey Gitomer*

Patterson established the first quota system used. When he established the system, it was a relative number based on the salesman's territory. It was a reflection of what the salesman should be able to bring in based upon the wealth of his territory. Back then and still today, quotas are a system to measure the **minimum** standard of achievement.

Here's a rule I created. It's called: The Rule of **The More The More**: The more you believe, the more you will sell. The more value you provide to others, the more people will come to know and respect you. The more you study sales, the more you will know how to react to any sales situation. The more you cold call, the more you will know how to master the science of thinking and responding creatively. The more you follow up, the more sales you will make.

Reach GOALS, not quotas.
Think being BEST, not quotas.

What is keeping you from reaching your quota? Reaching goals? Being the best?

If you were a Boy Scout, your motto was "Be Prepared." Your dad and mom drubbed into you your whole life, "do your homework." This was not an exercise. Rather it was a lesson. Doing your homework never ends. You did it in school. Now you must do it in business, or lose to someone who did.

Max Gitomer, my dad, always went into a sales call with a yellow legal pad full of homework, and almost always left with the sale. I wonder if there's a correlation. Homework by definition is "work" that you do at "home." That means turn off the TV and turn on the Internet. That means reading instead of watching. That means thinking instead of drinking. It means preparing which will lead to winning.

If you execute the fundamentals to the BEST of your ability, goals get met, and quotas get blown away.

Exercise: List the five fundamental things you need to do every day that will assure that you make a sale. Repeat them each day no matter what.

32.5 If It Has Been Working for 100 Years or More, Don't Even Think About Changing It.

"There is nothing new under the sun but there are lots of old things we don't know."

— *Ambrose Bierce*

"If you want to learn something new or get a new idea, read a book that's seventy years old."

— *Jeffrey Gitomer*

Tradition is everywhere. Football rivalries that go back over 100 years. Democrats vs Republicans, any religious ceremony, holidays, and parades. And people are attracted to, and attracted by tradition. They fly thousands of miles to participate. They talk about it. They compare it to last year or years gone by. Patterson's principles, strategies, and ideas are no different.

The reason things have been around for 100 years is that they have been working for 100 years. Family traditions like Thanksgiving dinner, or the Italian seven-fish dinner on Christmas Eve, etiquette traditions like thanking people and welcoming people (without the use of a computer), and personal financial traditions like saving or investing a percentage of your income. They are so traditional that they are irrefutable. If you can identify the traditions of your business and become a master at them, you will not only be successful, you will also be respected.

Tradition is a sacred, powerful insurance of success.

THE TRADITION OF
THE 100 POINT CLUB

The 100 Point Club (now the Century Point Club) was started for salesmen who sold 100 points per month. Each register was appointed a specific point value. To qualify, any salesman in the NCR American Selling Force who secured 100 points per month any time after January 1, 1906, qualified as a member. The insignia of this exclusive club is a solitaire diamond mounted on a solid gold star; the star being emblematic of the high standard of salesmanship, and the gem of the quality of his ability. This club still meets nearly 100 years later. That's tradition.

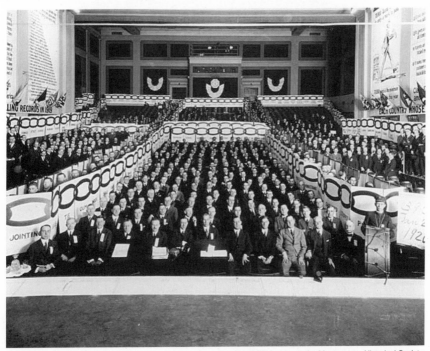

The NCR Archive at the Montgomery Historical Society

CPC convention, 1920.
John Patterson front row, second from right.

The benefit was an all-expense-paid, two-week convention in Ohio with the officers of the company. Patterson started dangling hefty rewards for those who exceeded their sales goals. Some rewards were as large and grand as a new car. Every reward was carefully calculated to grasp the desire of the salesman. Only merchandise of the highest quality was given. All NCR salesmen were working for something beyond salary and commission. They had something extra to strive for, in turn producing a hard-working, goal-achieving, and dedicated salesman.

"Loyalty Produces Leaders" was the motto adopted by the members of the 100 Point Club during their first annual convention. This motto explains how the men who attended the convention gained the high honor of being the leaders of the American selling force.

The 100 Pointers are loyal

1. To their company

2. To their company's methods

3. To their own ideas of high-class salesmanship

4. To good business practice

5. To yourself

The 100 Point Club was a celebration, an acknowledgment, and a learning experience. Almost 100 years later, the 100 Point Club is still alive. Very alive.

I have had the privilege and the honor of addressing that group at their convention. It was a thrill and a challenge to do my part of providing new knowledge.

Traditions are a valuable asset and a link to success. They link the past with the present. They help you see what has been done. They help you remember what to do. And they give you the confidence you can do it because it's been done before.

Traditions are there for you to learn from and embrace. They are there to help you succeed.

CPC parade in downtown Dayton in the snow, c1920.

"Reward those who have helped you succeed with a public display of appreciation."

— *John H. Patterson*

"People will try to rain on your parade because they have no parade of their own."

— *Jeffrey Gitomer*

TRADITIONS OF SUCCESS AND PRINCIPLES FOR LIFE

If you are a 120-year-old company, you've got tradition. Lots of it. There are things you have kept and enhanced over the years. Two big ones at NCR are *The Primer* (sales training manual that started in 1887) and the "CPC" or Century Point Club (sales awards and recognition that began in 1906).

Some traditions get eliminated that in retrospect you realize or wish you had kept.

NCR had a magazine called *The Hustler.* (See inset at right.) It started in 1884, and for some reason was eliminated. Its purpose was to communicate ideas, news, and the successes of NCR. These days, when people think of *Hustler* magazine, a more risqué offering comes to mind. But in its day, *The Hustler* was depicting what Patterson wanted the salesperson to do: *hustle.*

The NCR Archive at the Montgomery Historical Society

The Hustler magazine

Part of selling is moving quickly (hustling), and in those days, it was all about getting from one place to the next as fast as they could. At the turn of the last century, they couldn't hop in a car and get to the next place. There were no cars in 1889. They had to catch the train to get to the next city.

A favorite book in my library is called, *The Fuller Bristler*. It's one year's worth of the Fuller Brush Company weekly newsletters, written by their own (door-to-door) salesmen. The salesmen referred to themselves as "pluggers." The first issue that year (1925) was a bunch of thoughts that were inspired by "pluggers." It was a way that salesmen (they had no women) could help each other.

They didn't have cell phones or e-mails back then to communicate. The newsletter was the only way they could connect and communicate. It was about sales techniques and ideas. It was about one salesperson sharing information and encouraging another salesperson.

That's the way it was in 1925. That's the way it's supposed to be. And that's the way it is in successful sales organizations.

It was no different at NCR. Magazines and newsletters were a traditional part of their sales support. But NCR went much further. Patterson's brilliance was that he would bring his salespeople together for a conference. He would make all of them show up *and* dress up. Subliminally he was saying, "All my guys look alike; therefore, they share the same problems." His brilliance was in his subtleties.

He taught them, he challenged them, he let them interface with each other, he communicated with them weekly, and he rewarded them for their success. In public.

And when you repeat that process year after year, it becomes tradition. A tradition of successfully repeated actions, deeds, and principles. You have won in the past, no reason you won't win today. And tomorrow. In other words: You win!

Flipchart -- Patterson (left) and Gitomer.

THE POWER OF A FLIPCHART

Is the flipchart a tradition? Patterson used one in 1900, and with all the technological advances, I still use one in 2004. It's still the best communication and idea-clarification medium I know. I bought my first one in 1972. (That's me on the right.)

Nineteen seventy-two was a breakthrough year for me. I was learning the science of selling. I was under-funded (ok, almost broke). And it's the year I got attitude.

The flipchart played an integral part in my decision making and my attitude achievement that year, but I didn't realize the power of it until 30 years later. All I did was put a bunch of things on the flipchart that told me what I had to do in order to attain a positive attitude and kept the flipchart open to the page until I did it.

Part of my training regimen was reading one chapter of Napoleon Hill's book each day. The book only has 15 chapters. And part of it was making sure I lived the attitude each day, even though my life was not in the best condition at the time. (Ever been in that situation?) The twins were just born, I was in a rotten marriage, and I was broke.

But when people came up to me and asked me "how it was going," I would say, GREAT! (and it was actually pretty crappy). I don't know if I still have that flipchart page. But I do know that I have saved about 50 of the flipchart pads over the years. The one thing I did preserve was my positive attitude. That will be with me until the last minute of the last day.

I always use a flipchart at the beginning of an idea or the beginning of a project. The flipchart defines and outlines ideas and concepts in a way that creates detail you hadn't thought of. As you write each point, it sort of spurs your mind to the next point and makes you say, "oh, yeah" while you write furiously.

Sometimes I copy the sheet on my laptop. Sometimes I tape several of the sheets on the wall as I brainstorm. But since I have already written it down, it's also subliminally in "the force" area in the back of my head.

How I execute it is through osmosis. I already have it down on paper. I am not good at detailed planning. But I'm good at thinking. I'm good at writing. And I am good at creating. The flipchart is the perfect medium for all three of those. It's big. It's blank. And it's conducive to a thoughtful, creative person. I have even gotten to the point where I am picky about the kind of markers I use on a flipchart.

Flipchart paper has impact. It's BIG. Lots of room for thoughts and ideas.

Flipchart clarifies thinking -- it extends thought.
Once you have written down what you are thinking -- it frees your mind to discover another thought or aspect of the plan or idea.

The flipchart clarifies thinking -- it extends thought -- and once you have written something down, the flipchart also communicates ideas and concepts. Every seminar I have ever done had a flipchart (even though I also have a PowerPoint presentation).

I love taking the flipchart, drawing a line down the middle, and asking the audience to yell out the biggest objections they get. "Price," "satisfied with present supplier," "takes the lowest bid," "won't return my calls," they scream. Same objections every time. A thousand seminars. Always the same objections.

Then on the other side of the sheet, I say, "Your product aside, tell me what your customer is trying to accomplish in his or her business." And they yell out, "make more sales," "keep customers loyal," "have greater productivity," "make profit." Same answers every time. A thousand seminars. Always the same answers.

Then I say, if you could make all things on the right -- the things the customer wants -- come true, would your objections matter anymore? The entire audience -- and now you -- say the objections would fade away. The flipchart becomes this huge AHA! by taking something that everyone already knows and structuring it in a way that people see it AND perceive it.

Flipcharts are cheap. They cost between $50 and $200 bucks. And some of you are wondering if the boss will buy you one. MAJOR CLUE: You have your own money now. And you can begin to invest it in the most important person in the world. You.

A flipchart is the perfect medium to make a concept transferable.

What's one idea worth? What's an idea that you capture worth? How many ideas have you ever had that you lost because you didn't write them down? The flipchart captures, communicates, expands, solidifies plans, and the flipchart preserves so that you can go back and see what you did and revise your plans.

The flipchart is not an option.

THE LEGEND OF THE 1904 WORLD'S FAIR

The NCR Archive at the Montgomery Historical Society

NCR exhibit at the 1904 World's Fair in St. Louis.

NCR had an exhibit at the 1904 World's Fair. John Patterson was shrewd enough to convince every concessionaire to purchase a cash register and issue receipts for purchases. This ensured Patterson ultimate exposure for his machines throughout the fair.

Every exhibitor was emphatic about visitors not touching their wares. "Do not touch" signs were everywhere -- except at the NCR exhibit. Patterson invited everyone to "touch." He encouraged people to try the machines and print receipts for themselves.

These actions are more proof of Patterson's winning sales strategies.

THE LEGEND OF 5 AND .5

If you ever get a chance to read *The Primer*, you will see that every time John Patterson made a point or created a rule, he would attach 5 points to drive it home. The transferability (in Patterson's case, the memorization process) of each of his points corresponded to fingers on your hand. And in many cases you would actually see an illustration of a hand and each example above a finger. A simple yet powerful technique.

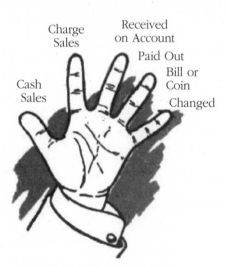

Charge Sales
Received on Account
Paid Out
Cash Sales
Bill or Coin
Changed

Hand from the 1919 Primer.

Sales folklore says that he liked the number 5 not just because it corresponded with fingers, but also because there were 5 types of money, there were 5 things customers would do when they walked into a store, there were 5 things he wanted his salesmen to do before they walked into an appointment, and many other examples that solidified the number 5 to John Patterson's legacy.

Patterson realized that the selling process was a science. He experimented, as any good scientist would, until he found formulas that worked. And then he repeated them. And got hundreds of his salespeople to repeat them.

It was the simplicity combined with the science that made the concepts transferable and successful.

In 1992 I was hired by another speaker to help him with marketing a new program on leadership. He was already an expert on time management and had established himself with hundreds of customers. My job was to create an additional learning program so he could go back to loyal customers who loved him and get more business.

I came up with a cool idea. I wrote the speech on leadership with eight points: Maintain a positive attitude, embrace change, deploy courage, take a risk, listen with the intent to understand, communicate to be understood, delegate and empower, understand yourself and your situation.

 I explained to him that these were simple and powerful leadership qualities but that there was no "glue." So I said, "Let's do 8.5, and make the .5 'commitment.' Because without commitment none of the other qualities will really make you a leader." I thought it was brilliant. But fortunately my client said, "I don't like it."

"No problem," I said. "Do you mind if I use it myself?" And from that moment on, every list I made (or ever will make) ended with the "glue" of .5. It has not only become a trademark, it has also become my most thought-provoking challenge that each time I make a list I make certain that the person who reads the list knows how to take the strategies and apply them to him- or herself.

What's the difference between 5 and .5? Why are they even relevant to this discussion? The answer is one word: transferability. In order for you to read, understand, incorporate, and succeed from these principles, you have to both get it and do it. And I promise you that if you get it and do it, you will also achieve the .5 -- bank it.

THE UNTAPPED POWER OF THE PROBABLE PURCHASER

Here's the challenge, Hoss: You've been referring to this prospect as a prospect for 20 years. Maybe some of you only two years. In your mind, you **must** begin the transition **from thinking** *"prospect"* to thinking *"probable purchaser."*

I'm an expert in selling. I believe myself to be the best at sales and the selling process in the world. I love the pitch. I love when a CEO that I'm presenting to gets up and walks around, and I go sit in his chair. I love when I can convince him to say the words, "My people need to have this." Or, "My people need to see this."

You know what that means? **The register rings.** Money.

I have studied the history of sales for 30 years. Every time I read something I learn something. I especially love reading books more than 50 years old because old ideas are usually new ideas, revised or in disguise.

When I began to study John Patterson, it changed many things about the way I thought sales should be conducted. And when I came across the words that Patterson used to define prospect, I believe it to be one of the five biggest AHA! events of my life. Not only was it brilliant, it was obvious.

He referred to the prospect as a **probable purchaser**. WOW!

I thought to myself, "Why doesn't everyone do that?" Some companies call them suspects, prospects, or defects. They're crazy. They're already setting a negative tone in your mind for what you think will happen.

Patterson, in his brilliance, set a positive tone for every potential customer that a salesperson would encounter by referring to them as a *"probable purchaser."* Nothing that I have ever seen in the realm of selling has even come close to that brilliance.

If you begin now to refer to **your** potential customer as a "probable purchaser," it will change your entire mental outlook as you enter the sale, while you make the sale, and when the sale is completed.

Once you have it in your mind, you will call them probable purchasers forever because that holds your key to self-belief and self-assurance. Your self-belief is half of your sales. It's the part that you can transfer to another person. They catch your passion, your enthusiasm, your attitude. And all of that comes from self-belief. And self-belief comes from your inner language. Using the term probable purchaser will lead you to more sales. I promise.

If you think of a
prospect as a prospect,
you are doomed to
the attitude of "maybe."
If you think of them
as a probable purchaser,
you will walk into
a sales call thinking, "Yes!"

HOW TO LIVE
THE PRINCIPLES

It's easy to read the principles and commit them to memory. It's easy to read these principles and say to yourself, "Yeah, I already know that." But that isn't *living* these principles. To live is to incorporate them into your life. They worked 100 years ago, and they still work today.

NOTE: Patterson was not distracted by a TV. Rather, he was distracted by family and books. To understand the Patterson model of success, it may be necessary to avoid or ignore the television for some period of time.

With each principle there is an exercise. By taking action, you are learning to live the principle. However, you can't just do them, you must master them. Master the actions and then you will live the principles to their fullest. It will take some time, and a great deal of self-discipline, but the end result will be profitable in more ways than you can imagine. Not just in sales. In life.

Please also note that I didn't say "do" the principles, I said "live" them. Exercise is combining "knowing" and "doing." Here's the formula: knowing + doing = living. It's so much more powerful when they are ingrained. **Here are 5.5 simple steps to "live" the principles:**

1. Read — Read to understand. Many people read to "confirm." They (not you, of course) read and think or say, "I know that." Knowing is NOTHING. It's asking yourself "how good am I at that?" that leads to a real understanding of the principle. Reading to understand is a deeper and more powerful read.

2. Think! — Think about how each principle translates to your career and your life. Think about how you could be more successful if you mastered each principle. Think about what it will take for you to do that.

3. Rate Yourself — Assess your present skill level for each principle. Mark the page at the top with a number between one and ten.

4. Plan Yourself — Let's say you rated yourself a six at principle number ten, Prospect for Probable Purchasers. What is your plan to raise your level of mastery to a nine at that principle? Make that plan, and put a deadline to start and a deadline to achieve.

5. Start Small, but START -- Select two principles that you have almost mastered. Figure out a way to improve on what you already have mastered. Then select two principles where you are not too good and figure out a game plan to get better at those. Most people are not good at what they don't enjoy. Your game plan to improve weaknesses should include how to have more fun in your weak areas.

"Fun" leads to improvement faster than "lessons."

5.5 Decide to Dedicate to the Self-Discipline to Succeed. All of this information is useless to the individual who reads it and does not act. The decision to act and dedication to follow through are the secrets. They don't sound like secrets. In fact, they sound obvious. Therein lies the flaw and the opportunity. Most people are looking for the easy way. Those people will be looking forever. You have an opportunity to pass all of those people, and most of the rest. All you have to do is decide to do so, and dedicate yourself to doing it.

Most people will not do the hard work it takes to make success easy.

Don't be like most people.

Put your heart into your business.

"You can not expect to be a success unless you believe whole heartedly in the value of your product. You interest people, first, by the thing you talk about; and, second, by the way you talk. Your talk will not ring true, your words will not carry conviction, unless you are thoroughly sold on the merit of your proposition. Believe in your goods. Be loyal to your Company. Put your heart in your work."

— *Excerpt from* The Primer, *1923*

RING THE REGISTER

The one-millionth cash register sold by NCR. Cha-Ching!

One hundred twenty years after John Patterson created the demand for a receipt, salespeople around the world all still live by the basic Patterson premise of: *ringing the register.* More interesting is the fact that I almost overlooked this premise, and were it not for a dinner with Pat Hazell at Sullivan's, this AHA! would not have been included. I showed him my book as he toured our studio and office and I told him a little bit about Patterson. He had just done a series of events in Dayton, and as we discussed the book a little bit, he asked if there was a chapter in it called *ringing the register.* And I just sat there thinking to myself, *cha-ching*, there isn't, but there will be.

Ringing the register is THE most fundamental aspect of a salesperson's process. If you do everything in the sales cycle, but you fail to ring the register, then as a salesperson you have failed. The register, and its accompanying receipt (aka the order), is the measure by which sales success or failure is determined.

You can throw any argument at me. You can throw any excuse at me. You can throw any sob story at me, but the fundamental question remains. Did you ring the register? Did you make the sale? And so the goal remains the same. Your company vision may be different. Your company mission may be different. Your company's product may be different. Your company's service may be different. The way you do your business may be different. But you all have the same goal. Ring the register. Make the sale.

Whatever John Patterson did or did not do. Whatever John Patterson was as a person or was not as a person. Whatever John Patterson's intention or vision was or was not, 120 years later the processes that he created or inspired others to create: the word think; calling the prospect a probable purchaser; the first sales training manual; the first quota system (yeah, you have Patterson to thank for your quotas); sales territories; an emphasis on testimonial advertising and selling; the training of salespeople in a boot camp; the reward to salespeople for a job well done; the celebration of victory on an annual basis; and of course, the receipt, arguably still the most powerful document in our economic society; these incredible leadership actions and principles still cast a shadow and are still at the core of any businesses success and every salesperson's success.

Every time a register rings a salesman gets his wings.

And so I challenge you to go back and begin with principle one, Think! And day by day, principle by principle, master each of these strategies and calls to action. And toward your success, and toward your fulfillment, understand that the goal will always remain: ring the register, baby. Ring the register.

Cha-Ching!

THE PATTERSON PRINCIPLES OF SELLING

1. *Think!*

2. Self-belief ... The Most Convincing Characteristic of a Salesperson.

3. Positive Mental Attitude Is Determined by You, Not Others.

4. Boot Camp Separates the Salesman from the Wanna-be Salesman.

5. Survival is a Combination of Knowing and Doing.

6. Studying ... the First Discipline of Knowledge.

7. Your Library Is the Artesian Well of Knowledge.

8. Planning Prevents Wandering and Provides Direction.

9. Use "Today Time Management."

10. Prospect for Probable Purchasers.

11. Increase Business Connections to Increase Sales.

12. Creating the Demand Converts Selling to Buying.

13. A Prepared Demonstration Means Personalized!

14. Gain Interest with Information about the PP not the We-We.

15. Questions Lead to Answers. Answers Lead to Sales.

16. Listening Leads to Understanding.

17. Less Sell-Talk Time Leads to More Buy-Time.

18. Your Message Must Be as Compelling as Your Product to Engage the PP.

19. An Objection is the Gateway to a Sale.

20. Selling is Not Manipulating; Selling is Harmonizing.

21. Complete the Sale with an Agreement to Buy … and Be Certain to Give Them a Receipt.

22. Service is the Reputation for the Next Sale.

23. Extra Service Leads to the "Testimonial Word."

24. Referrals are Better Earned than Asked for.

25. Testimonials Will Sell When the Salesman Can't.

26. Advertising Brings Awareness. Testimonial Advertising Brings Customers.

27. Competition Means Prepare to Be Your Best.

28. Recognize and Thank Those Who Have Helped You Succeed.

29. To Get Loyalty, You Must GIVE Loyalty.

30. Decide … It Doesn't Matter If It's Right or Wrong … Decide.

31. You Become Known by the Actions You Take. Take Ethical Actions.

32. If You Have Done Your Homework and Prepared Well, It Will Be Evident in Your Sales Report Card.

32.5 *If it has been working for 100 years or more, don't even think about changing it. Tradition is a sacred, powerful insurance of success.*

AUTHOR'S BIOGRAPHY

JEFFREY GITOMER
CHIEF EXECUTIVE SALESMAN

Photo by Mitchell Kearny

AUTHOR
Jeffrey Gitomer is the author of *The Sales Bible* now in its 18th printing, and *Customer Satisfaction is Worthless -- Customer Loyalty is Priceless.* Jeffrey's books have sold more than 350,000 copies worldwide.

OVER 100 PRESENTATIONS A YEAR
Jeffrey gives seminars, runs annual sales meetings, and conducts training programs on selling and customer service. He has presented an average of 115 seminars a year for the past ten years.

BIG CORPORATE CUSTOMERS
Jeffrey's customers include NCR, Coca-Cola, Cingular Wireless, Hilton, Choice Hotels, Enterprise Rent-A-Car, Cintas, Milliken, Financial Times, Turner Broadcasting, Comcast Cable, Time Warner Cable, HBO, Ingram Micro, Wells Fargo Bank, BMW, Baptist Health Care, Blue Cross Blue Shield, Hyatt Hotels, Carlsburg Beer, Wausau Insurance, Northwestern Mutual, Sports Authority, GlaxoSmithKline, Ricoh U.S., A.C. Nielsen, IBM, AT&T, Caterpillar, and hundreds of others.

IN FRONT OF MILLIONS OF READERS EVERY WEEK
His syndicated column *Sales Moves* appears in more than 90 business newspapers, and is read by more than 3,500,000 people every week.

AND EVERY MONTH
Jeffrey's column appears in more than 25 trade publications and newsletters. Jeffrey has also been a contributor and featured expert in *Entrepreneur* and *Selling Power* magazines.

HOST OF SELLING POWER LIVE
Jeffrey has been chosen to be the host of *Selling Power Live!*, a monthly one-hour program distributed to thousands of subscribers. The CD contains world-class experts interviewed by Jeffrey, followed by a Gitomer insight or strategy. There is also a full-page ad each month in *Selling Power* magazine promoting the subscription with Jeffrey's picture and credentials.

ON THE INTERNET
His three WOW websites -- *www.gitomer.com*, *www.trainone.com*, and *www.knowsuccess.com* get as many as 5,000 hits a day from readers and seminar attendees. His state-of-the-art Web-presence and e-commerce ability has set the standard among peers, and has won huge praise and acceptance from customers.

UP YOUR SALES WEB-BASED SALES TRAINING
A weekly streaming video (low cost -- high value) sales training lesson is now available on *www.trainone.com*. The content is pure Jeffrey -- fun, pragmatic, real-world, and immediately implementable. This innovation is leading the way in the field of e-learning.

SALES CAFFEINE
A weekly "e-zine" sales wake-up call delivered every Tuesday morning to more than 100,000 subscribers free of charge. This allows us to communicate valuable sales information, strategies, and answers to sales professionals on a timely basis.

SALES ASSESSMENT ONLINE
New for 2003 is the world's first customized sales assessment. Renamed a "successment," this amazing sales tool will not only judge your selling skill level in twelve critical areas of sales knowledge, it will give you a diagnostic report that includes 50 mini-sales lessons as it rates your sales abilities, and explains your customized opportunities for sales knowledge growth. Aptly named KnowSuccess -- the company's mission is: *You can't know success until you know yourself.*

AWARD FOR PRESENTATION EXCELLENCE
In 1997, Jeffrey was awarded the designation Certified Speaking Professional (CSP) by the National Speakers Association. The CSP award has been given less than 500 times in the past 25 years.

BuyGitomer, Inc. • 310 Arlington Avenue Loft 329 • Charlotte, NC 28203

www.gitomer.com • 704/333-1112 • salesman@gitomer.com

ACKNOWLEDGMENTS AND THANKS

To the research and editing team of: **Rachel Russotto**, **Amanda Desrochers**, and **Laura Miller**: ... Thank you for sharing in my excitement for this book, and for your insight, research, and your weekends. This project would not have been possible without your constant hard work and "prodding."

To **Adam Sakoonserksadee** for the powerful and provoking cover designs. Award-winning design is rare. And appreciated.

To **Greg Russell** for an 11-year friendship and a heroic and masterful job of typesetting this manuscript. It embraces the content and makes the words jump off the pages into your eyes.

To **Mitchell Kearney**, a world-class photographer, for capturing my image in spite of my hair.

To the **NCR Senior Management Team** ... Thank you for being my customer and for supporting this project. And thank you for standing on tradition and continuing to believe in and implement John Patterson's principles.

To **Barb Swinger**, of NCR: Thank you for your professionalism, your patience, your input, and your corporate insight. You are not only a pro, you are cool.

To the **Montgomery County Historical Society**: ... Thank you for access to your extensive archives, and thank you for your cooperation.

Research material used to find and corroborate facts and philosophies:
Selling Suggestions: Book Two, Efficiency in the Business, Frank Farrington, 1913
The Sales Strategy of John H. Patterson, Roy W. Johnson and Russell W. Lynch, 1932
John H. Patterson, Pioneer in Industrial Welfare, Samuel Crowther, 1926
Builders in New Fields, Charlotte Reeve Conover, 1939
He Who Thinks He Can, Orison Swett Marden, 1908
NCR News, Various editions, 1922-1927
The Primer, Various editions, 1889-1923

Photos from the NCR archive at the **Montgomery County Historical Society**.

NOTES

NOTES

NOTES

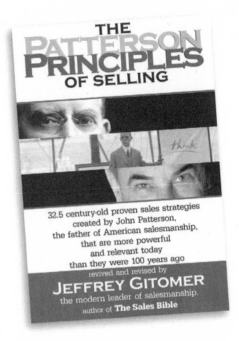

Want *The Patterson Principles*
for your sales team?

Want to become a certified
Patterson Principles presenter?

Want to add *The Patterson Principles*
to your training business?

We have developed a complete Patterson Principles training
program that features Jeffrey Gitomer's live seminar
(available online or CD-ROM)
and a classroom learning package that assures
lesson transferability to your business.

Call 704.333.1112 or e-mail patterson@gitomer.com